MW00483161

Any Body There?

Any Body There?

Worship and Being Human in a Digital Age

Craig Mueller

WIPF & STOCK · Eugene, Oregon

ANY BODY THERE?
Worship and Being Human in a Digital Age

Copyright © 2017 Craig Mueller. All rights reserved. Except for brief quotations in critical publications or reviews, no part of this book may be reproduced in any manner without prior written permission from the publisher. Write: Permissions, Wipf and Stock Publishers, 199 W. 8th Ave., Suite 3, Eugene, OR 97401.

Wipf & Stock
An Imprint of Wipf and Stock Publishers
199 W. 8th Ave., Suite 3
Eugene, OR 97401

www.wipfandstock.com

PAPERBACK ISBN: 978-1-5326-1916-8
HARDCOVER ISBN: 978-1-4982-4531-9
EBOOK ISBN: 978-1-4982-4530-2

Manufactured in the U.S.A.   JUNE 19, 2017

All Scripture quotations from the New Revised Standard Version Bible, copyright © 1989 Division of Christian Education of the National Council of the Churches of Christ in the United States of America. Used by permission. All rights reserved.

"Come to Us, Creative Spirit." Words by David Mowbray. Copyright © 1979 Stainer & Bell, Ltd. (Admin. Hope Publishing Company, Carol Stream, IL 60188). All rights reserved. Used by permission. Reprinted under license #78453.

"O My Lord, If I Worship You" from Women in Praise of the Sacred: 43 Centuries of Spiritual Poetry by Women, edited by Jane Hirshfield. Copyright © 1994 Jane Hirshfield. Reprinted by permission of HarperCollins Publishers.

"Whatever Is Seen in Joy" from This Day: Collected & New Sabbath Poems, by Wendell Berry. Copyright © 2013 Wendell Berry. Reprinted by permission of Counterpoint.

Contents

Acknowledgments

I OFFER THANKS TO the people of Holy Trinity Lutheran Church, Chicago, for the opportunity to use my deeply rewarding ministry there as the impetus for academic study and reflection, and later for the writing of this book.

Special thanks to Richard McCarron, my thesis director, for his guidance and support during the writing of my Doctor of Ministry thesis; and to Mark Bangert, academic advisor, mentor, professor, and choral director when I was a student at Lutheran School of Theology at Chicago in the 1980s—who offered insight and support during the writing of the thesis.

I am grateful to the following colleagues who offered critique on individual chapters of this book: Philip Anderson, William Beermann, Dave Daubert, Jack Finney, Kent Mueller, Theresa Nollette, and David Nelson. I extend deep appreciation to Erin Bouman for detailed feedback on multiple chapters, and especially to Carol and Ryan LaHurd, who carefully edited the entire manuscript and offered inspiration every step of the way.

Most of all, I thank my spouse, Ernest Vasseur, for his enthusiastic support and hours of proofreading and for the many hours we have shared discussing my earlier thesis and this book; and my parents, Gerald and Delores Mueller, who modeled faithfulness to congregational worship and supported my lifelong passion for liturgy and the church. *Soli Deo Gloria.*

Introduction

"ANY BODY THERE?" WE may shout that question when we enter an empty house. One of my friends recently pointed at my head and asked, "What's going on up there?" I couldn't tell whether he was making sure I was paying attention or he wanted to know what was on my mind.

"Is *anybody* there?" I hear that question when I think of today's religious landscape. Pews are sparsely filled these days. Churches are closing and religious institutions of all kinds are wondering what the future holds for them. Fewer people are going to church than several decades ago. And those who are attending are going less frequently. In a day when spirituality is *in*, even churchgoers have weaker ties to the institutional church than their parents and grandparents did. We are told that churches and denominations will look different in the future. What that means more specifically is mere speculation. Surely people will continue to practice the Christian faith, but in structures and formats we may not recognize today.

"Is any *body* there?" I hear that question in yet another way. These days many of us are so tethered to our electronic devices that they seem to be extensions of our bodies. I am not an expert in anthropology, but I wonder if what it means to be human is changing. We are becoming more like our computers, and computers are becoming more like us. With so many distractions, how often are we fully present in and to our bodies anymore?

It is not only our devices that are online. Our brains seem to be connected to the Internet as well. It is harder to live in the present moment. When our attention is scattered, what is most often sacrificed is our relationships with the people right next to us, not to mention our relationship with nature and the earth. It reminds me of a cartoon in which Dilbert confides in a friend

1

whose attention is on his smartphone: "Everything went wrong for me this week. I have problems . . . all kind of problems." The friend glances toward Dilbert and then returns to his phone while saying, "For the zillionth time in a row, my phone is more fun than talking to a human."[1]

The Body and Being Human

Any body there? The body is the guiding image for this book. To be human is to have a body. We experience life's greatest joys and pleasures in our bodies. Our deepest pain and loss are most often the result of our bodily mortality and finitude.

In this book I will explore what it means to be human—to be embodied—in a digital age. In our individualistic culture, many people adopt a personalized spirituality as a way of seeking meaning. I will argue, however, that true meaning comes from communal, religious ritual that accentuates what it means to be human and marks the rhythms and life passages of everyday life. Rituals have been intrinsic to the human story for millennia. And they nearly always connect us to some aspect of our embodied reality. It is certainly possible for people to create their own rituals for their personal lives, but will they? Will parents have the time and energy to devise rituals for their children?

Despite the remarkable ways technology enhances our lives, today's digital culture is at the same time leading to further disembodiment and fragmentation. This book builds on a Christian anthropology that unites mind, body, and spirit in the human person. My reflections will be grounded in an incarnational and sacramental spirituality that recognizes the presence of God in daily life. You may be asking, "Why are you so fixated on the body?" Isn't religion about so-called spiritual things?

A Body Spirituality

The body was irrelevant to my faith as a child and a teenager. I believed that the body was the problem. Authentic Christianity was about the soul. Since college the body has grown more integral and vital to me. Embodiment is now the unifying and core conviction of my faith.

---

1. Adams, "Dilbert," 14 July 2016.

Along with cultural, technological, theological and liturgical insights, I will share stories from my own life. That means at this point I need to say that I am gay and many of my personal vignettes come from my experience as a gay man. Undoubtedly, coming to terms with sexuality and one's body is complicated for all of us. Coming of age in the 1970s, I faced the added confusion of being gay and what that meant for the call I felt to pastoral ministry. Since I am a private person and because gay relationships were deeply controversial until recently, telling these stories is another part of a lifelong process of coming out. Perhaps these vignettes will help you, the reader, understand the significance of the body to my spirituality.

Furthermore, the body can be considered theologically in so many ways. I love this about Christianity. Our bodies are the first and most important gift from God—the very means we have been given to carry out our unique vocations in the world. Certainly, the stewardship of our bodies ranks as one of our most important callings. In the Eucharist we partake of the body of Christ for spiritual sustenance and nourishment. Finally, the body of Christ also refers to the community that gathers for worship and then scatters for service in the world. All of these are the *body of Christ*: our bodies, the bread of the Eucharist, and the community itself.

Why are bodies so important to Christian spirituality? Why does *matter* matter? Isn't religion about things of the soul? Consider two central tenants of the Christian faith: creation and incarnation. Let's begin with the scientifically verifiable fact of our embodied existence. In the Genesis creation story God declares that the material world is *very good*. God breathes into humanity the breath of life, and the human person is created in the image and likeness of God. This could not be further from the all too common religious understanding of an amorphous soul separate from than the body. A Hebraic understanding of humanity clearly suggests a unity of the person. I like the way Old Testament scholar H. Wheeler Robinson used the term "animated body" to speak of the Hebrew idea of the person, as opposed to the Greek concept of an incarnated soul.[2]

The incarnation—God sharing our flesh in Jesus Christ—gives Christians further reason to honor and take seriously our bodily existence. Early Christians spoke of the incarnation as heaven wedded to earth. Certainly one could say that God is spirit. Yet, for Christians, divine love is concretized in the fully human and embodied life, death, and resurrection of Jesus Christ. The incarnation declares that God is with and among bodies that

2. Murphy, "Human Nature," 20.

are frail and strong, sick and well, weary and energetic. To declare that the "Word becomes flesh" is to offer the highest esteem to our embodied state as human beings.

It is not only the body of Jesus that is holy, though. All human bodies are holy. Yet a long history of dualistic thought has led many Christians to seek a salvation of only the soul and a devaluing of the material world. In such reasoning, getting saved is not a bodily experience. A soul is saved, departs the body at death, and will eventually live with God forever. Clearly this belief in the immortality of the soul does not reflect the Judeo-Christian scriptures and tradition. Paul, for example asserts that there is no resurrection without the body (1 Cor 15).

It may seem more plausible to imagine bodiless souls floating through eternity than the Christian belief in the resurrection of the body. Since bodies decay, cremation is increasingly accepted. Many think the afterlife, then, must be made up of souls living on, even as bodies die. The problem with this line of thought is a devaluing of our present bodies. No wonder, then, that in many places today such little attention is given to the body at the time of death.

As a result of the Enlightenment and centuries of mind-body dualism, we largely educate seminary students from the neck up. One negative effect of this is that spiritual leaders often encourage people to think of themselves as souls or spirits, even though their daily experience belies this approach. If every second of our lives is lived in and through our bodies, how do we even speak of experiencing our souls? If, as I have been arguing, human beings are not a separate shell of flesh harboring a disembodied soul, what are the implications for spirituality and worship? I will explore liturgy in which all the senses are used and the incarnation is celebrated in and through the bodies of the assembly. Rather than an escape from the body, I argue for a spirituality that locates salvation in our bodies and advocates care for the body through diet, exercise, rest, and recreation.

Though technology brings great opportunities and creative possibilities, it can also disconnect us from our bodies, from the earth, and from each other. One can certainly have spiritual experiences on the Internet, yet they are usually disembodied and individualized. Our gadgets can distract us from being fully present to one another. They can distract us from noticing the sky, the sun, and earth.

To center one's spirituality on the body of Christ provides balance to the virtual realities we experience online. Though one can read Scripture, pray, and reflect alone and with a computer, the reception of the Eucharist is in real time and necessitates the community we call the body of Christ. To suggest that Christian worship is not simply reflecting on the meaning of spiritual truths but an encounter with an embodied assembly is counter-cultural. It requires continued effort to refute the common understanding that salvation is merely personal and not necessarily bodily. Granted, one can be "spiritual, but not religious" in countless ways, but here I will explore what it means to gather in a community of bodies, using senses, symbols, gestures, and sacraments. Rather than one wondering if we *have* a soul, I would rather ask whether our worship has soul, and whether our worship gives witness to what it means to be human.

I propose that amid a steady decline in mainline denominational affiliation and a simultaneous increase in the use of digital technology, corporate worship is a life-giving antidote to the distraction, restlessness, and spiritual hunger in contemporary life. Participation in the Sunday liturgy accentuates what it means to be human: a deeper connection to our bodies and the earth, and a clear sense of purpose and mission in our everyday lives. As a means to accomplish this task, I will reflect on the intersections of contemporary culture and Christian spirituality.

Spiritual, Religious, and What It Means to Be Human

I have loved going to church since I was a young child. Though my faith has continued to change throughout my life, I continue to gravitate to the liturgy as a source of spiritual renewal and formation for life. Many people today assert that they are spiritual but not religious, viewing religion as hypocritical, judgmental, or irrelevant. Others insist that they are religious and not spiritual, concluding that the latter is undefined, irrational, and not connected to a time-tested tradition. This book is about being both spiritual and religious. I have been in many conversations that have attempted to discern the difference between two terms. Usually it comes down to spirituality being about experience, meaning, and one's relationship with God. For some, religion is the problem, especially when rules and rituals, structures and scriptures, are experienced as restrictive. For others, the downside of spirituality is when it becomes a rationale for individualism and freedom from the confines of a religious tradition. Throughout the book a question at the back of my mind is this: Does going to church make any difference in our lives?

I will advocate that participation in corporate worship deepens the spirituality of those who participate, and opens up meanings and connections with what it means to be human. One might expect that someone like me—a pastor—would make the case that it is important to attend church. True enough. My main argument, however, is not primarily that the future of the institutional church is at stake—though it clearly is. Rather, I believe with all my heart that liturgy *is* spiritual formation. Even if the benefits are not always conscious, going to church opens our hearts to the great mystery of death and life. Few other gatherings in society consistently put before a community such a rich menu of spiritual themes: that we are embodied and mortal, that we need relationships and community, and that we seek meaning and purpose for our lives.

My reflections arise out of my ministry at Holy Trinity Lutheran Church in the Lakeview neighborhood of Chicago, where I have served as lead pastor since 1999. Holy Trinity has experienced steady growth in the past eighteen years, including hundreds of young adults in their twenties and thirties. An assumption is sometimes made that young adults want worship that is high-tech, with projection screens for song lyrics and praise bands for musical leadership. In my context the reverse is true. These urban millennials talk about the importance of tradition. They may spend little time away from technology, yet they respond to the note in our worship bulletin that says, "Help us create SACRED SPACE by powering down." And though the congregation is known for social activism, the event that consistently that draws the largest number of people is worship.

Path Forward

This book draws on research from my Doctor of Ministry thesis, but takes a more practical approach. It weaves narratives from my life and ministry, especially among millennials, with examples from digital culture and a variety of theological insights. Each chapter is organized around a theme from technology that defines our lives, in lesser or greater ways.

Chapter 1. *Virtual: Reflecting on Bodies and Technology*

> The book begins with our complicated relationship to our own bodies while exploring the importance of embodiment to Christian spirituality. How do our digital lives affect the conviction that we know God most fully through incarnational and sacramental experiences of daily life?

Chapter 2. *Icons: Imaging Bodies*

We interact with icons everyday on our computers and smart-phones. In Orthodox Christianity icons are windows to the divine. As we locate the divine presence in the bodies of Jesus, Mary, and the saints, how can multisensory worship reminds us that our bodies are icons, signs of the holy in all of human life?

Chapter 3. *Analog: Acknowledging Mortality*

We live in a digital world defined by numbers and algorithms. Our bodies, however, are analog, limited by illness, suffering, and death. How can the rituals of Ash Wednesday and funerals deepen our awareness of our own mortality and the mystery of death and life?

Chapter 4. *24/7: Finding the Time*

No one seems to have enough time in our 24/7 world. How can worship as a spiritual practice remind us of the importance of rest and renewal and form in us a different sense of time?

Chapter 5. *Design: Seeking Beauty*

We respond not only to the functionality of our devices; we value the design—and the sleekness—of many products. If worship has to do with the beauty of God, can liturgy open our eyes to beauty in our own lives and transform us into people of gratitude and praise?

Chapter 6. *Access: Welcoming Mystery*

We have digital access to more information and resources than we could ever use. If access is also a way to talk about how the church welcomes newcomers, how can our encounter with strangers—indeed, with all that is *other* to us—assist us in welcoming mystery into our lives?

Chapter 7. *Connectivity: Embracing Real Life*

Social media allows us to be connected with others online. How might we consider preachers as reflectors-in-residence who assist their hearers in nurturing significant meaningful connections with God while pondering the joy and suffering of daily life?

Chapter 8. *Selfie: Striving Toward Community*

Selfies are ubiquitous. While society is becoming more individual-ized, what are the benefits of communal worship and participation in a faith community?

Chapter 9. *GPS: Mapping Purpose*

While we rely on GPS to get us from one place to another, we may
wish we had clear directions as we struggle to find our purpose in
life. At the end of the liturgy we are sent forth to live our faith in
the world. Can participation in worship help us to discover and
affirm our vocation?

Chapter 10. *Augmented Reality: Being There*

In the concluding chapter I will bring the various spiritual themes
together as I reflect on what *being there* means. Using an Eastern
approach to mindfulness, I will discuss being in the moment, being at church, and being in the world. In this digital age, I can
think of no more important question: What does it mean to be a
human being? In a time of much doing, how can we learn to *be*? It
is the spiritual question of our time.

1

Virtual

Reflecting on Bodies and Technology

WHAT DOES IT MEAN to be embodied in an increasingly digital culture? Before we consider our contemporary context, think about the relationship we have had with our own bodies over the years.

Maybe nobody feels good about their body when they are a kid. I sure didn't. I gravitated toward the piano and not to the outdoor sports that most other boys were playing. Thus, I was particularly lousy at baseball, football, and basketball—the big three, as I call them. I dreaded P.E.—physical education—more than anything. The *physical* part meant it had to do with the body. My dad tried to play catch with me. I was required to take swimming lessons no matter how hard my strong-willed personality protested. Looking back, though, I don't think I was very comfortable in my own skin—with and in my body. I'm sure each of us will have our own story from adolescence and how it affected our sense of body image in some way.

It's not an exaggeration to say that P.E. led me to God. Before bed, I would kneel down and pray that I could make it through another day of class, especially when we were in a unit of one of the big three. After all, most boys had developed skills from hours of practicing and playing these sports. For me, it was simply humiliating. Whether or not anyone made fun of me, I would have rather been reading, making music, or doing anything less competitive, and less bodily. Add to that a kind of Christian faith that seemed to privilege soul over matter, and it's easy to see why by the age of twelve I didn't think the body mattered much. The world itself was filled with sin. Better to strive for the higher spiritual plane untainted by bodiliness. Eventually we would go to heaven—a better place—in which our souls at last could be set free from our sinful bodies. At least that is what I believed then.

After all, sometimes bodies fail. My mom was stricken with polio in high school and throughout her life she lived with bodily limitations and losses. Even vacuuming took effort for my mother, so when we were young my brother and I would help with such rather simple household chores. When we vacationed in Disneyland, we walked the whole day while she traveled the park in a wheelchair, though she normally didn't use one. And there was the day I will never forget when she slipped on a step at the front of the church while returning from Communion. I can still remember her crying on her bed when returning home, a poignant scene of vulnerability I had rarely seen.

Puberty brings body issues for everyone. When you don't think the body is as important as the soul, sexual awakening may bring even more guilt and ambivalence. But then if you find yourself attracted to people of the same gender, everything gets so, shall we say, complicated, as it did for me. I would find myself spending time with girls, not because I was physically attracted to them, but because they understood me. And I clearly wasn't going to get any of them pregnant, despite the concern I heard at home. With the natural bodily urges that came during these years, I would just try to do as the song in the Broadway musical *The Book of Mormon* says: "turn it off like a light switch." So when I was drawn to boys, it was my heart that confused me. I tried, for a while at least, to rationalize away my bodily desires.

It's been the work of a lifetime for me to reunite body and spirit, as if they ever were two entities. It has certainly included coming out, forming relationships, and eventually getting married to a man. I have come full circle from myself as a teenager, now valuing materiality and the body as the essence of what it means to be human, and therefore the basis for an incarnational, sacramental Christianity. I note now how many of my favorite, renewing activities are very bodily, such as running, yoga, meditation, cooking, and eating.

The Missing Body

There is no escaping the body, however hard we try. Even when seeking our so-called higher nature, eventually we are brought back to bodies that demand food, drink, and rest—not to mention additional care when we face illness, pain, stress, or the effects of aging. Advertisements give us nearly constant messages hoping to convince us that the use of certain products will keep us young, attractive, fit, and otherwise happy. Many of us have complex relationships with our bodies throughout our lives. Some would go so far as to blame long-held philosophical and theological dualistic thinking, in part, for such lifelong problems and challenges. Several theologians, however, make the point that we don't simply have bodies, we are bodies. They use the term *body-selves* to express this reality.[1]

These days, though, I wonder if our virtual and digital experiences are causing us to become even more disembodied. But before we go there, we need to name the dualism that still resides in our psyches, despite the psychological, spiritual, and religious advances made in the past several decades. For no less than the past thousand years Western Christian thinkers have sought to favor the higher soul over the mortal body. Theologian Colleen M. Griffith describes the "missing body" in the human search for transcendence. "High-tech rationality has begun telling people that they do not need to worry about the body anymore; it can be transcended by technology. At the same time, consumerism is promoting an alternative body that it has produced, one that can be sold even better looks, more vivaciousness, increased appeal and freshness."[2] We could question how such dualism has continued to affect the struggle many people have with body image. We continue to hear that Americans are overweight and solutions vary widely, from urging more exercise to controlling portion size, eating less red meat, and cutting down on sugar or fat. Add eating disorders, such as bulimia and anorexia, and we begin to see a picture of a nation with a complex relationship to both food and bodies.

We also have an educational system that generally trains minds while ignoring bodies. In a widely viewed TED talk, Ken Robinson, a popular expert on creativity, laments that we consistently favor literacy over creativity. We educate people from the neck up—mostly the brain, and one side of it—holding up university professors as the apex of learning. They (and we, for the most part) live in our heads. Robinson quips that many people in academia act as if their body is simply a form of transportation for their heads, a way of getting their minds to the next meeting or intellectual endeavor.[3]

---

1. Hefner, Barreto, and Pedersen, *Our Bodies Are Selves*, Kindle loc. 81.
2. Griffith, "Spirituality and the Body," 69.
3. Robinson, "Do Schools Kill Creativity?" TED Talk.

In our educational systems, students can let off steam through activities like sports or dance, but for the most part physicality is deemphasized. I can see how this has been true throughout my education. Seminaries today are trying to balance more practical—and often bodily—wisdom that comes from real life experience with the theoretical approach at the core of the academy. Since the Enlightenment, at least, we have raised the mind to an even higher plane and relegated the body to something almost outside ourselves, attending to it when we are hungry or tired, for example. Guy Claxton, professor of learning sciences, argues that we turn to the world of ideas since bodies are seen as "fallible, corruptible, and irrational . . . Reason is our highest and most precious achievement, the pinnacle of intelligence, and sober rationality brings us nearer to the divine, while the body drags us down to the world of beasts and beastliness."[4]

Are We Losing Touch?

I am glad that there has been a return to the body in a number of disciplines, including spirituality and theology. For a number of years there has been talk of uniting body, mind and soul, though behind that equation is an assumption that those are separate things. A question for our time is whether our virtual lives are making us even less embodied and threatening some essential aspects of being human.

Philosopher Richard Kearney tells of discussions with his college students regarding their experiences of finding potential sexual partners through various digital matching services. These relatively anonymous encounters are usually void of flirtation, courtship, seduction, or even caress. The way to get connected to a body for sex often does not actually include the literal presence of a body, but merely online profiles and pictures. Kearney could not help note the striking paradox: "The ostensible immediacy of sexual contact was in fact mediated digitally. And it was also noted that what is often thought of as a 'materialist' culture was arguably the most 'immaterialist' culture imaginable—vicarious, by proxy, and often voyeuristic."[5]

In a turn of phrase of particular interest to sacramental Christians, Kearney speaks of *excarnation* to describe our contemporary context. What appears to be our current obsession with the body is actually making us

4. Claxton, "Corporal Thinking," 19.
5. Kearney, "Losing Our Touch," August 31, 2014.

alienated from our actual bodies. Normally we describe the incarnation as the Word becoming flesh. If we consider the Word or *Logos* to be an image of invisible God (Col 1:15) then perhaps we could join Kearney in describing the incarnation as the image becoming flesh. *Excarnation*, which marks our digital age, is flesh becoming image. In this case, image refers to disembodied representations on screens. Kearney argues that both Puritanism and pornography are alienated from the flesh, "one replacing it with the virtuous, the other replacing it with the virtual."[6] Whereas Aristotle considered touch as the entry point to all our senses, Western society went with a Platonic emphasis of sight over all the other senses. Kearney argues that this led to two thousand years of optocentrism, "culminating in our contemporary culture of digital stimulation and spectacle. The eye continues to rule in what Roland Barthes once called our 'civilization of the image.' The world is no longer our oyster, but our screen."[7] In Kearney's view, a proliferation of screen images prevents us from experiences in the flesh, in our bodies.

Those are challenging words to hear. In church we talk about being created in the image of God. In a positive sense, images and icons can represent and reveal a deeper presence, as we will explore in the next chapter. Yet we must ask: Is our ubiquitous use of screens, and the images on them, leading us away from our bodies and multisensory experiences? Or can one's personal presence be truly mediated through a digital encounter? A fascinating topic, indeed, so let's go there, at least briefly.

Virtual Identities

Rachel Wagner, who studies religion and culture, especially virtuality, defines "virtual reality" as "any form of digital technology that involves user engagement with software via screen interface."[8] Though people use their bodies when using technology—eyes looking at a screen and fingers typing on a keyboard, for example—to what extent is virtual engagement an experience of the body or not? Do these forms of communication and activity lessen our connection to our body-selves and to the earth? These emerging forms of virtual reality are certainly the wave of the future. Though many simply celebrate technological advances, are there deep concerns that need to also be named?

6. Ibid.
7. Ibid.
8. Wagner, *Godwired*, 1.

The anonymity of the Web provides an avenue for us to express a part of ourselves not revealed in real life as these parts take on screen names that may or may not match our everyday personas. Not only can we exhibit different personalities in chat rooms and other online venues, we may present ourselves by means of a different age, occupation, income level, nationality, or even gender. The Internet gives us a sense of control. Though online anonymity seems liberating, it is easy to forget that what is put on the Web is both public and permanent, and colleagues, job recruiters, and others can access the information and use it in a way that has negative implications for us.[9] A lack of inhibition allows us to create an online personality and say things behind a screen that we never say in real life. We may feel free to speak freely, often without thinking or editing.[10] At the same time, this anonymity may allow some of us who are living a false life in the real world to truly be ourselves in the virtual world.

Creating an e-identity can be exciting and provide a sense of adventure and risk that one may not be experiencing in everyday life. Psychiatrist and author Elias Aboujaounde studies obsessive-compulsive disorder and behavior addictions, with particular focus on the Internet. He notes that "unfettered by old rules of behaving, social exchange, etiquette, or even netiquette, this virtual personality is more assertive, less restrained, a little bit on the dark side, and decidedly sexier."[11] Online pursuits may prompt us to buy something we cannot afford, or present ourselves as thinner or more successful than we really are. Whereas these darker aspects of human nature were traditionally "kept in check by culture, religion, and what one might call the social contract," Aboujauounde believes that this new way of presenting ourselves to the world is nothing less than a revolution equal to the Industrial Revolution.[12] As inhibitions lessen, we may gain a false sense of our grandiosity, a narcissistic view of ourselves, and an impulsivity without the needed checks and balances.[13]

For some, confusion may arise when moving between one's virtual and everyday selves. Though past generations have opined about the dangers of each technological advance—such as radio and television—Aboujauounde believes the Internet can indeed intrude dangerously into our

9. Small and Vorgan, *iBrain*, 51.

10. Rosen, *iDisorder*, 10–11.

11. Aboujaoude, *Virtually You*, 20.

12. Ibid., 21–22.

13. Ibid., 43.

everyday lives. "Its immersive and interactive qualities, how it can talk back to us, engulf us, break us down and then reconstitute us into something different—all distinguish it from other waves of technology that have caused panic over the decades, and all make it so that there might be more at stake today."[14]

Gifts in Our Virtual Lives

I share many of the concerns listed above, yet I realize these realities are nuanced; I do not want to be purely negative in my thinking about virtuality. Several writers make intriguing points by comparing religion and virtual reality and noting that both are concerned with the *other*, that is, the possibility of transcendence. Consider religious scholar Rachel Wagner and her book *Godwired: Religion, Ritual and Virtual Reality*. Despite the decline of organized religion in America, Wagner notes that human beings are creative; and virtual reality provides "secular forms of ritual that offer us meaning, imaginative engagement, enchantment, and temporary escape from our ordinary routines."[15] Despite the concern that online activity is disembodied and can become addictive, Wagner wonders if our fascination with virtual realities is a result of our "disillusionment with the postmodern, the fragmented, the uncertain." Perhaps our desire for the virtual has a religious quality to it as we seek meaning and order for our "own real lives." If religion is imagining a different world, and if it "is about stories that animate our lives, rituals that shape our consciousness, and modes of interacting that define who we are, then it seems to me that virtual engagement is doing some of the very same things."[16]

Is there a way in which virtual experiences could be considered "embodied"? Theologian Sheila Briggs contends that human beings tend to see the body as "the dwelling of the self" despite the body-negative messages we have received from our religious and philosophical traditions.[17] Briggs wonders whether digital technology, coupled with our imaginative potential, can provide a transformed vision of human corporeality.[18] She challenges the assumption that online endeavors are not grounded in real-

14. Ibid., 286.

15. Wagner, *Godwired*, 7.

16. Ibid., 14.

17. Briggs, "Digital Bodies and the Transformation of the Flesh," 157.

18. Ibid., 160.

ity and suggests that digital technology can "provide our imagination new resources for envisioning and planning our rapidly advancing future."[19]

Finally, sacramental theologian Daniella Zsupan-Jerome points out that just as our personal presence is mediated digitally apart from a physical body, the presence of Christ, in a sense, is mediated to us in the Eucharist. This eucharistic presence correlates with the absence of Jesus' literal body following his resurrection and ascension and leads to a present-day encounter with the communal body of Christ. For Zsupan-Jerome, it is possible to experience someone's true presence (and essence) without being together face to face, but that does not mean we should normalize such encounters that dismiss or transcend the body.[20]

For example, though couples may meet each other online, it is not until they meet in person that there is truly a sense of attraction or compatibility. A true sense of openness to the other person, even experienced digitally, will make "room for the full, mysterious complexity of the other person as truly other."[21] In this ideal encounter we are in a "posture of seeking and recognizing the person behind the screen, who is both revealed and concealed by the symbols of their presence: the pixelated word, the digitized image and sound. Without this intentional posture we are merely reacting to digital artifacts on the screen, objects that can fill our gaze like (an) idol, and objects that can draw out from us flippant, cutting, and violent words in response."[22] As mysterious and exciting as our digital encounters may be, they ideally should lead to truly embodied experiences in the flesh. If one uses the term *virtual* to speak of Jesus' presence in the Eucharist, there must be caution so that human physicality is not diminished. An assembly of bodies sharing food and drink continues to be the locus of the divine presence for the Christian community.

Looking to the Future

I often contend that we are becoming cyborgs. Is what it means to be human changing in our digital age? When our smartphones are nearly an extension of our bodies, and we are connected to the Internet more than we are not, I wonder what the next stage of human evolution will bring. I

19. Ibid., 157.

20. Zsupan-Jerome, "Virtual Presence as Real Presence?," 539.

21. Ibid., 539.

22. Ibid., 542.

do notice that my concerns are rarely matched by those of my nephew and niece, and others a generation or more younger.

To N. Katherine Hayles, a postmodern literary critic, our bodies in the future may evolve into "data made flesh."[23] Information would become more important than materiality. Human embodiment would seem an "accident of history, rather than an inevitability of life."[24] Hayles contends that if the body is the "original prosthesis we learn to manipulate" then the body can become something that can be "seamlessly articulated with intelligent machines."[25] Whether imagining such a future stirs up terror or excitement, religious leaders and communities will need to grapple with the implications of humanity morphing more and more into cyborgs. When Hayles imagines a world inhabited by so-called posthumans, her nightmare is that they would "regard their bodies as fashion accessories" rather than their very essence. Her dream is they would not be seduced by "unlimited power and disembodied immorality," but recognize and celebrate the limit of human mortality and finitude and understand that we live in a "material world of great complexity, one on which we depend for our continued survival."[26]

How will we reflect ethically on these new realities? I was delighted to find a posting on "Transhumanism" on the website of the Lutheran Alliance for Faith, Science and Technology.[27] There was a brief interview with Phil Hefner, a retired theology professor who taught one of my seminary classes several decades ago. In discussing something called "Transhumanism," Hefner notes a potential use of science to "extend life indefinitely and eliminate all the ills that beset us, as well as achieving 'perfect' bodies." As much as many of these goals distort the human condition, at least from a theological perspective, there are positive goals as well, such as curing disease.

Hefner believes that God has created us with the potential to "push the envelope" of what it means to be human, yet we must also be cognizant of the "omnipresence of finitude, arrogance, greed, and other aspects of sin." In other words, a theological response to Transhumanism names the ambiguities and possibilities, the greatness and degradation possible from such endeavors.[28] It is always challenging to guard what human so-

23. Hayles, *How We Became Posthuman*, 5.

24. Ibid., 5.

25. Ibid., 2.

26. Ibid., 5.

27. Lutheran Alliance for Science and Technology, http://luthscitech.org.

28. Hefner, interview with Susan Barreto.

ciety considers essential or normative while being open to new concepts that improve our lives in significant ways. These final words from Hefner cause me to reconsider some of my initial discomfort with some of these ideas. "We like to think of human nature as something solid, reliable, and even unchanging . . . Many Christian critics of Transhumanism seem to be caught up in hostility to the mystery and the awesome potential that God has given us. At the same time, we must not deny that we are also finite and sinful."[29] Sorting through the risk and potential in the Transhumanism realities named above will demand significant discernment from all segments of the human community, including those representing religious and theological perspectives.

Back to the Body

Amid speculation of how human beings will relate to their bodies in the future, I am going to call us back to the wonder of our bodies, frail and mortal as they are. As I reflect on our lived experience in our bodies, both in church and in our everyday lives, I am delighted to be a sacramental Christian that insists on the unity of body and soul. Embodiment not only grounds my theology and pastoral ministry, it is also the essence of my spiritual life. Christian liturgy is grounded in the goodness of creation and the incarnation, that is, the Word become flesh. Not only do we partake of the body of Christ in the Eucharist, we use St. Paul's metaphor of the body of Christ to describe the Christian community. In the next chapter I will consider the body as an icon for the divine, and look carefully at the role of the body in liturgy. There is no escaping the body, whether in our human experience or within the heart of Christianity itself.

29. Ibid.

SPIRITUAL PRACTICES

1. When churches discuss stewardship, the emphases usually include time, talent, and financial resources. How can communities of faith encourage care for the body as an essential spiritual commitment?

2. Many people would likely describe spiritual practices as things that are good for their soul—such as prayer, meditation, and reading Scripture. How can we expand our definition of spiritual practices to include activities that renew the body as well? What might you include as embodied spiritual practices in your life?

3. In *Praying All Ways*, Ed Hays broadens a definition of prayer to include the use all the senses. Perhaps some of his book's chapter titles could inspire creativity in your own prayer life: Praying with the Eyes, The Prayer of Tears, Praying with the Nose, Praying with the Feet, Play as Prayer, The Prayer of Napping, Feasting as Prayer.[30]

30. Hays, *Pray All Ways*, 7.

2

Icons

Imaging Bodies

WE INTERACT WITH ICONS everyday. On computers, smartphones, tablets, and newer televisions, we click on an icon to open up a program. As I look at my iPhone home screen, I instantly identify icons for the calendar, phone, and music programs. Each app features a carefully selected symbol: a bell for the meditation app, a wrapped present for an app that lists birthdays and anniversaries, a smiling orange for Fooducate, a simple lowercase "f" in a blue background for Facebook.

In a larger sense, icons have to do with branding. Institutions invest significant financial resources in designing logos that will be instantly recognized. Art historian Martin Kemp examines our age of celebrity icons and frenetic company and cultural branding in his book *Christ to Coke: How Image Becomes Icon.* He begins with the images (icons) of Christ and the saints in Christianity, and then traces the process of the following becoming iconic images: the heart (as in "I♥NY"), the MGM logo with a lion, the *Mona Lisa*, the Stars and Stripes, Coke (the bottle and the beverage), and several more.[1]

The proliferation of images on television, in advertising, and on the Internet leads some writers to suggest that the image is superseding the word in the everyday life of Americans. For example, there has been a shift in homes from libraries to family rooms, and from bookshelves to entertainment centers,[2] and of course now to mobile phones and computers.

1. Kemp, *From Christ to Coke*, xiii.
2. Stephens, *Rise of the Image*, 5.

Leonard Shlain asserts that the rise and fall of literacy has resulted in a present-day return to an image-based society. He believes that the iconic revolution that began in the nineteenth century is linked to feminine values—thus less patriarchal, resulting in more balanced expressions of religion and spirituality.[3]

My own reading patterns bears this out. I find myself skimming quickly over columns of text but being drawn to linger over a photo or infographic. Many preachers now use projected images or short video clips in sermons. My congregation's weekly e-newsletter uses headline banners with only a few words and an image since we realize people read less carefully today. For example, a wine tasting event may picture filled wine glasses and the date and time with more information revealed if you click on the headline banner.

Since liturgy makes use of symbols, bodily gestures, and participation, the gradual move from word to image is interesting to consider in light of the renewal of sacramental worship. Do the images on our screens enable us to appreciate an incarnational spirituality, or do they lead to a disembodied *excarnation*, as one author quoted in the preceding chapter argued? At this point let me clarify that when I speak of incarnation, what I mean is close to what some theologians define as "deep incarnation." The concept of deep incarnation expands the particularity of God's incarnation in Christ to all of creation. The entire materiality of humans, animals, and plants—including the suffering of sensitive creatures—is full of divine grace.[4]

In this chapter I will briefly consider the use and meanings of icons in Christianity, discuss how the incarnation is an icon of the divine, and reflect upon the implications for bodies created in the image of God. From this perspective, we will take an in-depth look at the use of the body in a liturgical setting of sacramental worship.

Religious Icons

The study of icons was the focus of a study trip I made to Italy and Greece. Earlier my spouse and I had vacationed in Turkey for several weeks and I became fascinated with the Byzantine architecture and art in churches from the fourth through the thirteenth centuries. In Eastern Orthodoxy, icons refer not only to the small, portable images that we usually think of,

3. Shlain, *Alphabet Versus the Goddess*, 4–7.
4. Gregarsen, ed., *Incarnation*, 361–80.

but also to the mosaics and frescoes on the walls and apses of churches. In all of these, the representations of Jesus, Mary, and the saints are stylized, with a consistent, recognizable form. The icons are not simply art. They serve a spiritual or devotional purpose for the faithful. "Above all, icons show us the Incarnate God, the materials of the image becoming a channel between two worlds." Like a two-way mirror, grace is approached and channeled. Just as the gospel is communicated through words, an icon reveals religious truths through symbols and forms.[5]

When we were in Greece we noticed Orthodox Christians use their bodies to bow in front of icons, make the sign of the cross, and kiss them. The icon makes present Jesus, Mary, or the event portrayed in a sacramental kind of way: a physical sign of something spiritual. Sometimes icons are described as doorways to the holy. Whereas Western religious art may portray a biblical scene or express a devotional sentiment, icons in Eastern Orthodoxy are meant to lead to a sacred encounter with the saint pictured. They provide an "entry into the presence of the holy."[6] Though many Roman Catholics and Protestants may not have this particular experience of icons, these days it is not uncommon to see one or more icons in churches of many denominations.

On our trip I marveled at glittering mosaics in Ravenna, Rome, and Venice, especially in the Basilica of St. Mark. I loved seeing the frescoes painted on walls of the dozens of churches throughout Greece. Classic scenes—the nativity, the baptism of Jesus, the transfiguration, the dormition (the falling asleep) of Mary, and many others—were portrayed in similar ways and places in the various churches. In early centuries of church history the faithful learned the central stories of Christianity through their encounters with icons.

Icons point to the incarnation, the presence of God in human bodies. In fact, all icons portray bodies, not isolated symbols such as a cross or dove. A key relevant Scripture passage is "Christ is the image [Greek: *icon*] of the invisible God, the firstborn of all creation" (Col 1:15). Orthodox priest Simon Ckuj notes, "Praying with icons is an ancient prayer practice that involves keeping our eyes wide open, taking into our heart what the image visually communicates. We focus not on what is seen in the icon,

5. Martin, *Sacred Doorways*, 13.
6. Ibid., 231.

but rather on what is seen through it—the love of God expressed through God's creatures."[7]

Like sacraments, icons point to a deeper spiritual reality beyond what is first experienced with our bodies. In the same way that icons always include a human figure and could be described as body images, in liturgy "the human body is a privileged place where we know and name God. The much-maligned body is, in fact, the sanctuary where we *meet* and *welcome* the Holy One in our lives. For after all, in the Christian economy, we meet the Divine in the daily, the holy in the human, the eternal in the everyday."[8]

The Body in Liturgy

Without the body—our physical reality as an icon of the divine presence among us—there is no liturgy. For theologian Louis-Marie Chauvet, the purpose of liturgy is not to pass on ideas and concepts, but to be a corporeal experience: "that which is most spiritual thus comes only through the mediation of that which is most corporeal."[9] This is challenging for those who think the purpose of worship is predominantly to speak to our minds and hearts. Recent cognitive research is challenging the common assumption that our brain is like a conductor of the body and its systems. "Now the body is being revealed as a single dynamic system in which nerves, stomach, skin, and lymph are all in constant conversation with the brain. The body *is* the brain."[10]

All of this challenges the critique that ritual is simply going through the motions. In faith formation actions speak louder than words. Watch young children respond to the various bodily gestures and rituals in the liturgy. In my congregation there is not a children's sermon since Sunday school offers lessons connected to the lectionary, and the multisensory liturgy itself provides many ways of engagement for children. Each Sunday there are processions to watch and the bread and wine of Communion to receive. On the Sunday before Lent the children help ritually bury the word *alleluia* (written out on small banners) in a large chest that represents a coffin. On Palm Sunday children and adults vigorously wave palm branches during the entrance procession. On Christmas Eve, Epiphany, and the

---

7. Ckuj, "Praying with Icons," para. 4.
8. Mitchell, "Trinity of Themes," 75.
9. Chauvet and Lumbala, eds., *Liturgy and the Body*, viii.
10. Claxton, "Corporal Thinking," 19.

Easter Vigil, youth and older children read or even act out some of the readings. Small votive candles are lit near photographs of deceased loved ones on All Saints Sunday.

Liturgical theologian Ron Anderson writes of faith being written on the body as the liturgy "works subconsciously *in* us and *on* us to shape us in ways of acting, knowing and being in the world . . . pointing to what musicians and athletes understand well: the habits of liturgy written on our bodies intend and enable continued spiritual growth and formation."[11] How interesting that in Orthodox terminology icons are not "painted," but "written." Anderson argues that what we experience with and through our bodies may be deeper than what we can actually put into words; the liturgical actions may be affecting us in ways we may not even cognitively recognize or understand.[12] In liturgy we come to know the presence of God and the truth of our human story, and through repetition week after week "the liturgy starts to 'write' its meaning in and on our bodies."[13]

In my past studies on liturgy and the body, I was surprised that there were few books with this particular focus. I was excited to read the recently published *Embodied Liturgy: Lessons in Christian Ritual* by liturgical scholar Frank Senn. He speaks of his own "return to the body" when he faced colon cancer, and he weaves in his own experience with yoga throughout the book. In his exploration of a wide variety of bodily themes and practices in the liturgy, Senn makes the theological point that if God is going to transform our minds, that change must occur through our bodies. "That is the role and impact of the sacraments on the body."[14] In that sense, worship that is focused only on music and preaching is deficient in use of the senses, "because it doesn't offer sufficient visual, olfactory, taste, and tactile stimulation. Worship in which the worshipers are primarily seated is kinesthetically deficient because the body likes to be up and about—especially young bodies."[15]

Martin Luther insists that the liturgical meal of Holy Communion is not merely a spiritual experience, but a corporeal one: "all who break this bread, receive, and eat it, receive the body of Christ and partake of it. As we

11. Anderson, "Liturgy: Writing Faith in the Body," 173.

12. Ibid., 174.

13. Ibid., 177.

14. Senn, *Embodied Liturgy*, 8.

15. Ibid., xii.

have said, it cannot be spiritual, it must be bodily participation."[16] The word of God—for Luther, the proclamation of the gospel—is not merely words, but is joined to "the material world of water, wine, bread, and bodies."[17] Thus, the liturgy reveals that the bodily experience of being human is the very means to the spiritual.

For years I have taught how the body is involved in the liturgy by describing how all five senses are involved. It is an interesting exercise to name the senses and consider how each is employed in worship. Since many churches do not use incense (though I would encourage greater usage of this ancient practice), the nose often gets shortchanged, other than the occasional scents of flowers or candles. Likewise, it can be challenging to consider the sense of touch, but I also include general bodily postures, gestures, and movements in this category.

When I think back to my formative memories of Lutheran worship when I grew up in the 1960s and 1970s, bodily participation was limited to standing, sitting, and kneeling for Communion. There were few other bodily gestures in the liturgy; pastors presided by holding a book and reading words from a page. The word *ritual* had a negative connotation, and many contemporary embodied liturgical practices were considered *Catholic* then. Use of the senses in worship consisted of hearing the word and music, and seeing stained glass windows, cross and candles, altar and pulpit hangings in liturgical colors, and occasional banners, usually featuring large text. Since the word was preeminent, sacramental practices were minimalistic: a few drops of water for baptism, and a wafer and a small, individual glass of wine for Communion. What mattered most was what one believed in the mind, or perhaps felt in the heart. Doctrines and ideas about God and the faith were the marks of the Christian life. The senses were irrelevant.

Thanks to an ecumenical liturgical renewal movement, the expression of worship has changed considerably in the past several decades, not only for Lutherans, but for many denominations. There was not a particular moment in which theologians, pastors, or lay people suggested a more embodied liturgy; rather, it was a gradual process. Today, sensory sacramental practices and liturgical actions are more common in many congregations. Most of those listed below would be standard liturgical practice in most Roman Catholic or Episcopal churches, yet many items listed have been

16. Luther, "Against the Heavenly Prophets," 181.
17. Bieler and Schottroff, *Eucharist*, 132.

recently recovered or introduced in many Lutheran congregations and some Methodist, Presbyterian, and other Protestant denominations:

- Sign of the cross
- Bowing
- Kneeling
- *Orans* position (outstretched arms)—for worship leaders, occasionally for the assembly
- Processions (including gospel and offertory processions)
- Greeting of peace
- Eucharist with real bread
- Generous use of water at baptism (and possibly immersion)
- Imposition of ashes—Ash Wednesday
- Procession with palms—Sunday of the Passion/Palm Sunday
- Footwashing—Maundy Thursday
- Veneration of the Cross—Good Friday
- New fire—Easter Vigil
- Sprinkling with baptismal water
- Baptismal remembrance at the font
- Anointing with oil—baptism, healing
- Laying on of hands—absolution
- Use of incense in processions or evening prayer
- Use of chasubles for presiding ministers
- Icons (borrowed from Eastern Orthodoxy)

Embodied Liturgy

In worship human bodies participate in a variety of physical gestures, rituals, and sacramental actions that engage the mind as well as the bodily senses. As Christ is the icon of God, the body of Christ is now the icon of God's presence among us. *Body* takes on multiple meanings. The community is the body of Christ, using St. Paul's metaphor in 1 Corinthians 12. I have sometimes preferred to use the short phrase "the body of Christ" when distributing Communion bread. Not only is the bread the body of Christ, the person receiving the bread is also the body of Christ. In other words, our bodies become the locus of divine presence in the world. A tagline of the Evangelical Lutheran Church in America also makes this clear: "God's work. Our hands."

Since the Sunday morning liturgy is the primary gathering of the community, I will proceed through the service, using *Evangelical Lutheran Worship*, noting the various bodily gestures and actions. Though there is general ecumenical consensus regarding the overall structure and pattern that I will name, the specifics of various practices or ceremonial actions vary among denominations and among individual congregations.

The liturgy may begin with either **Confession and Forgiveness** or **Thanksgiving for Baptism**, and in both cases the assembly makes the sign of the cross over their bodies, remembering the gift of baptism. In the prayer of confession, the people may kneel as a sign of penitence and humility. In **Thanksgiving for Baptism**, the bodies of the assembly may be sprinkled with water from the font, the tangible droplets providing a reminder of baptismal grace on our bodies. When water is kept in the baptismal font, worshippers may dip their hands in the water to remember their baptism, making a cross on their forehead or their body.

During the **Gathering Song** the entire assembly may enter singing, but more common would be an entrance procession of the ministers, and perhaps the choir. This bodily movement—often led by cross, torches, and lectionary book—may suggest the baptismal journey from death to life. If incense is used in the procession, it adds the bodily sense of smell and is carried "before the cross, as if to signal 'the fragrance that comes from knowing [God]' and the 'aroma of Christ' (2 Cor 2:14–15) spreading in procession throughout the world."[18] Another bodily gesture treasured in some communities, a simple bow, may be used by the ministers or choir before the cross, table, or both. A bow offered by one or more ministers toward the assembly honors the presence of Christ in the community as well. "Of course, since the American Revolution, Americans rarely bow to anyone, perhaps rightly wanting instead to guard their equality. But perhaps Western Hemisphere Christians, in the assembly, could learn from Asian Christians about the deep significance and courtesy of a bow. Honoring others in this way can be a sign of Christian mutuality."[19]

18. Brugh and Lathrop, *Sunday Assembly*, 128.
19. Ibid., 129.

Greeting the congregation, the presiding minister extends hands in a posture of welcome and mutuality. During the **Prayer of the Day**, the presiding minister uses the ancient *orans* prayer posture of outstretched arms. This bodily gesture of "open arms—formed like an empty chalice or like a cross, open to the sky but also to the community—is widely found in images from ancient Christianity."[20] After the prayer, the assembly will sit, a posture of listening to the **Word**, until it stands again to greet the presence of Christ in the reading of the **Gospel**. When there is a **Gospel Procession**, additional bodily movement occurs as the congregation turns to follow the cross and torches that may lead the lectionary book as it is carried into the midst of the assembly. The congregation will again sit to listen to the **Sermon**, and then stand as the posture appropriate for the **Hymn of the Day, Creed** (when it is used) and intercessory **Prayers**. The assisting minister may also use the orans position for the prayers, and during Lent some communities kneel here as well.

During the **Greeting of Peace** the assembly offers a bodily gesture—a handshake, embrace, kiss, or even a bow—as a sign of Christ's peace. Another procession—or bodily movement—occurs as gifts of money, bread, and wine are carried forward. "All of these, including ourselves and our bodies, are the good things of the earth that God has made and given to be shared."[21] The presiding minister may use a gesture of greeting and a bow as the **Great Thanksgiving** begins, and then assume the orans position through the thanksgiving at table. In some communities, the assembly also uses the orans gesture during the **Lord's Prayer**. The assembly comes forward to receive bread and wine, yet another bodily procession. The sacramental action of eating and drinking is likened to a meal in which the community feasts on bread and wine, the body and blood of Christ.

Finally, during the **Sending Song** a cross may lead the final procession as the community is sent forth in mission. As the presiding minister blesses the congregation, the assembly may once more make the sign of the cross on their bodies. In all the above examples, the Sunday liturgy involves more than ears listening or minds reflecting on theological or moral lessons for life. Rather, human bodies walk, move, stand, sit, bow, kneel, listen, speak, sing, see, hear, touch, smell, and taste. The body is celebrated as a gift of creation and honored as sign and reminder of the incarnation of Jesus Christ.

20. Ibid., 134.
21. Ibid., 198.

The Body of Christ for the World

The human person is nourished not only by the body of Christ through partaking of the eucharistic bread and wine, but is also joined to others in the community and becomes the body of Christ in the world. Recent liturgical texts make a strong correlation between receiving the body and blood of Christ in the Eucharist and living as the body of Christ in the world. The term *epiclesis* refers to the invocation of the Holy Spirit in the eucharistic celebration. Though earlier Christian debates centered on when and how the bread and wine of Communion became the body and blood of Christ, recent texts make clear that the Holy Spirit is poured out on the community that it may become nourishment—bread—for the world.

This transformation of the assembly into the body of Christ is linked to an epiclesis that prays that the Holy Spirit will both bless bread and wine and will also enliven the people of God to live as the body of Christ in the world. Ron Anderson compares numerous ecumenical eucharistic prayers and notes that many recent ones make explicit "our request that consecration and communion not only benefit the individual recipient but the world."[22] Anderson names his fondness for Augustine's phrase "becoming what we receive." In other words, we are what we eat; yet Anderson also cautions that the effect is not based on our action, but is God's gift.[23]

As we become the body of Christ in the world, we will encounter the vulnerability and suffering of others. Following intercessions for those in need, the assembly greets one another with a bodily gesture during the greeting of peace. A Communion procession of bodies makes clear that we are all beggars, as Martin Luther said. In other words, these ritual moments reveal that mission is not only for the sake of those both inside and outside the assembly, but for all people who stand in need of mercy and compassion. The bread broken at the table calls the people of God to encounter broken bodies and broken spirits. Liturgical theologian Samuel Torvend links the Eucharist to the theology of Luther, connecting the physical act of eating and drinking at the Lord's Table to sharing the sufferings of others and serving those in need in a sacrament of love. Therefore, the social welfare of others is nothing less than a spiritual calling.[24]

22. Anderson, "Body for the Spirit in the World," 106.

23. Ibid., 114.

24. Torvend, *Luther and the Hungry Poor*, 113.

If the heart of the Eucharist is the broken body of Christ, the implications for ministry in daily life suggest an identification with those on the margins. According to theologians Andrea Bieler and Louise Schottroff, "those who are gathered around the table are the body of Christ in the world; their actual, individual bodies are temples of the Holy Spirit . . . Being the body of Christ in the world takes into account the fact that our physical bodies are porous: they are connected with the environment every second of our existence. The Eucharist is the feast of radical empathy with the most vulnerable."[25]

Bodies matter: those the church serves in the world, those in our pews, and those of worship leaders and pastors. It is to the latter that we now turn.

The Role of the Presider

It is a great joy for me to serve as presider at services of Holy Communion. Outside of church, I tend to my own body through exercise, diet, sleep, and yoga. I see all of these things as spiritual practices that reflect a stewardship of the body that God has given me. Yet, awareness of my own body is also central to liturgical presiding. Yoga poses, for example, carry over into the way I stand or move in liturgy. In fact, I would recommend yoga as a way for presiders—and others—to work with posture, alignment, and the general mind-body connection.

The presider's own bodily comfort and confidence will set the tone for others in the assembly. Robert Hovda, in a classic text on presiding in the liturgy, speaks of "the limits of verbalization, words, instruction, pedagogy" and the power of the "nonverbal, symbolic, body language of the liturgy."[26] The presider needs to "become a body person, at home in the flesh, moving gracefully and expressively, gesturing spontaneously, saying something to people by style in walking as in talking, communicating by the rhythm and articulation of the whole person."[27] How important it is for presiders not only to prepare well what they will say, whether the sermon or liturgical texts, but to plan, rehearse other participants, and lead well the various bodily movements, gestures, and processions of worship. Church of England priest Stephen Burns suggests that through art and its various forms, presiders should meditate on the body's graces. Burns reminds us that even when the presider

25. Bieler and Schottroff, *Eucharist*, 131.
26. Hovda, *Strong, Loving, and Wise*, ix.
27. Ibid., 31.

is idle, what he or she expresses with hands or eye movements is communicating something. Ultimately, we are seeking to embody a sense of reverence in liturgy: for our bodies, for the body of Christ, and for the bodies of the assembly. "There is, in fact, a whole repertoire of bodily *presence* to become alert to when it comes to presiding in liturgy: pouring oneself into a profound bow, paying real attention with one's eyes, being able to be still, depicting with one's hands what both giving and receiving might mean, yearning without saying a word, and so much more."[28]

Resurrection of the Body

If Christ is an icon of the invisible God, and our bodies an icon of this incarnate reality, one wonders why so many pay so little attention to the body in liturgy and in life. Samuel Torvend calls for a resurrection of the body in our congregations, in other words, "a "revitalization of the gestures, postures, and actions of the body in Christian worship, the Christian's imaginations, and Christian life in the world."[29] In making his argument, Torvend brings in fascinating insights by two early church fathers. First, Leo the Great (fifth century) preached that the "actions (*sacramenta*) of the Redeemer during his life on earth have passed into the life of his body through the actions of the church."[30] We now experience Christ's bodily presence through the actions that the church does in liturgical assembly. Second, Augustine suggested that there are "at least 300 *sacramenta* or sacred actions, at least 300 ways in which God communicates God's presence and grace through ordinary matter, through ordinary gestures, postures, and actions."[31] Though Roman Catholics name seven sacraments and Protestants two, there are considerably more bodily actions in worship that are signs of grace, many of them listed earlier in this chapter. Torvend has another reason for making this point, though. He believes "we live in a time when ecological theologians, Christian ethicists, feminist historians, New Testament scholars, pastoral counselors, and social activists are drawing attention to the human body, to earth's body, that is, to the mystery of the

28. Burns, "Yearning without Saying a Word," 12.
29. Torvend, "Touch Me and See," 24.
30. Ibid., 20.
31. Ibid., 20.

incarnation."[32] I celebrate this wonderful convergence of diverse voices calling us to embrace this essential mark of the Christian faith.

John of Damascus, an eighth-century monk, made the connection between icons and the incarnation: "I do not draw an image of the immortal Godhead, but I paint an image of God who became visible in the flesh."[33] He was countering the iconoclasts, who considered it blasphemy to represent God with an image. Yet since Christ was incarnate, icons also point to this reality. In other words, the body of Jesus, the bodies of the saints, and the bodies of the faithful today matter. Honoring bodies in worship teaches us to have reverence not only for our own bodies, but especially for those most vulnerable among us. A Jewish saying describes thousands of angels going before every human being, crying out, "Make way, make way for the image of God."

In a day when icons on screens often overshadow our embodied realities as earth creatures, the actions of the liturgy ground us in the human condition and bring us back to breath, water, oil, bread, wine, and the divine presence in the joys and struggles of daily life. Honoring bodies as icons of the divine, we may well want to seek a resurrection of the body: a renewal of embodied worship that helps the people of God to see and experience deep incarnation and all of human life as sacramental. In this sense, participating in worship forms us in the ongoing project of being human. An inescapable aspect of human reality is mortality, the topic to which we turn in the next chapter.

SPIRITUAL PRACTICES

1. Reflect on the liturgical practices in your worshipping community. Are all five senses involved regularly? Review the list on page 26 and consider implementing some of the actions and rituals not familiar to your congregation. Make the point that incarnational and sacramental spirituality is one important basis for the introduction of the new practice.

2. Learn more about icons in Orthodox Christianity and consider using an icon in your worship space or as a part of your individual prayer practices.

32. Ibid., 21.

33. Brubaker, *Vision and Meaning in Ninth-Century Byzantium*, 31.

3

Analog

Acknowledging Mortality

RECENTLY MY BROTHER AND sister-in-law had to put down a beloved dog they had lived with for only three years. My brother didn't expect that he would come to love the dog so much, and gets teary when talking about it. I got two black kittens in 1992 and when one of them, Berna, had to be put down in 2009 I could not believe all the tears that I shed. Never having had a domestic pet before, I soon discovered how common my experience is. Watching an innocent animal fail and then die unlocks all kinds of feelings. As one cat was dying, I would hold my other cat, Benna, a littermate, knowing her time was short as well. It was yet another bittersweet reminder that nothing is permanent in life, and that grief is the cost of love.

To be human is to know grief that at times feels inconsolable. Ritual is one way that we acknowledge the mystery of life and death with stark honesty. I am going to use the concept of *analog* to contrast the limits of our mortality with the digital lives we increasingly inhabit. These days we use *analog* as the opposite of *digital*. Analog is considered old school—things like vinyl records, typewriters, and clocks with hands and faces. Analog is imaged based, whereas digital refers to codes, that is, numbers. Whereas numbers are abstract, analog is based in physicality. If we see an analog clock divided into segments of the day, our brain translates the image into numbers. Not so with a digital clock: we skip this whole step.

Yet, human beings are not abstract. We are bodies created in the image of God, yet limited by illness, suffering, and death. After contrasting the human experience of loss and vulnerability with what we experience in our digital lives, I will describe how the liturgy of Ash Wednesday and the experience of a funeral with the body of the deceased present can assist us in more fully living within the gifts and limits of being human.

Crying seems to be one of the things that makes us human, something we share with very few other animals. People shed tears in all kinds of situations, but particularly in moments that stir up feelings of loss, mortality, and impermanence. At a funeral or in the midst of tragedy, for example, tears may reveal the depth of love and our helplessness in the face of human finitude. Perhaps one reason some people do not like autumn is that it stirs up melancholy and the reminder that, like leaves falling from the trees, our lives will have an end as well. One of my favorite poems, by Gerard Manley Hopkins, beautifully expresses this reality:

> Margaret, are you grieving
> Over Goldengrove unleaving?
> Leaves like the things of man, you
> With your fresh thoughts care for, can you?
> Ah! as the heart grows older
> It will come to such sights colder
> By and by, nor spare a sigh
> Though worlds of wanwood leafmeal lie;
> And yet you will weep and know why.
> Now no matter, child, the name:
> Sorrow's springs are the same.
> Nor mouth had, no nor mind, expressed
> What heart heard of, ghost guessed:
> It is the blight man was born for,
> It is Margaret you mourn for.[1]

Vulnerability and Loss

What I have learned through my own tears is that grief is cumulative. Though the process is often unconscious, I believe that each occasion of loss stirs up our previous experiences of grief and letting go, and those we anticipate in the future, whether in the short or long term.

My greatest experience of loss occurred in 2003 when I discovered that my long-term partner at that time was addicted to crystal meth

---

1. Hopkins, "Spring and Fall."

(methamphetamine). I thought his strange behavior was due to some kind of breakdown, but I soon learned of the power of the drug he was using, as it brought about not only the loss of his job, and of our life together, but a heart-wrenching challenge of untangling the condo and other assets we owned. He refused to cooperate in any way so I was forced to seek legal help. A judge's ruling a year later finally forced him from our condo, where he was then living. In essence, I had no other option than to cause my beloved of seventeen years to become homeless. There are no easy answers in trying to make sense of this tragedy. Even now it is hard to see how there is any redemption in this story, at least for my ex-partner, who had been a brilliant church musician and publisher, and is currently homeless and mentally ill. I remember sobbing, not only for my own loss, but for the waste of one human being's gifts and talents in what seemed and still seems a hopeless situation.

This unbearable loss—the worst thing that ever happened to me—led eventually to the most wondrous and joyful experience of my life. A new relationship began to blossom in 2007, resulting eventually in a liturgy of blessing, civil union, and finally an upgrade to marriage with the landmark Supreme Court ruling in 2014. Yet when feelings of vulnerability or the fear of being alone again get stirred up in me, I am aware of the earlier trauma that in some ways is still lodged in my body's memory. I do not talk about this story often, but I am certain that it defines me more than I know. As much as we may think of memories as mere images, what is more often triggered in us is an emotional response. I used to think of emotions as part of my mind's processing of information, but now many disciplines make clear that emotions lodge in our bodies—such as a knot in the stomach, tension in the neck, or sweaty palms.

When experiencing deep loss and naming dependence on God, we begin to embrace the limits of the human condition. Poet and philosopher David Whyte speaks from his experience of wistfulness and poignancy, noting the delusion we have that we can go through life without having our heart broken and the similar illusion that keeps us from facing the reality of our own demise. "To run from vulnerability is to run from the essence of our nature; the attempt to be invulnerable is the vain attempt to become something we are not and most especially to close off our understanding of the grief of others. More seriously, in refusing our vulnerability, we refuse the help needed at every turn of our existence and immobilize the essential, tidal and conversational foundations of our identity." The only choice we have, argues Whyte, is how we will "inhabit our vulnerability" and how it can lead us to live more courageous lives.[2]

Turning to Technology

I remember learning that God is omnipresent, omniscient, and omnipotent. Now anyone can be present anywhere and anytime through technology. Our virtual identity can be accessed in an instant on the other side of the world. With a smartphone in our hand, the Internet seems like an extension of our bodies. All we need to do is ask Siri or do a quick Google search and we have near miraculous access to unlimited knowledge. By observing what human beings have accomplished during the last century—in science, medicine, and technology—there seems to be no end to our power as well. "So what need is there for God?" some might ask. Human beings are on the verge of being omnipresent, omniscient, and omnipotent! No wonder one book on technology is called *iGods*.[3]

At the same time, we must come to terms with death, with human mortality and finitude, because whatever attributes of God we seem to be on the verge of acquiring, we are not on the verge of being immortal or infinite. The Buddhist notion of impermanence suggests that everything is illusion. Nothing lasts forever. By clinging less tightly to all that is passing away and by looking at what is truly real, we find true freedom and a new beginning. It may be human mortality and finitude that draws some people to spirituality even as technologies continue to evolve.

Digital Lives, Analog Bodies

I often wonder whether our evolving relationship with technology lessens our connection to the earth and our human limits. As devices become extensions of our bodies, we begin to use metaphors that suggest we are becoming machines. A friend mentioned the irony that the human brain that invented computers in the first place is now viewed as a form of the brain it invented. For example, in a dinner conversation when numerous topics have been briefly covered, I playfully mention that we have multiple files open. In the same way that we can recharge our phone at any time of

2. Whyte, "Conversational Nature of Reality," para. 108–9.
3. Detweiler, *iGods*.

the day or night, we begin to treat our bodies that way, seeing food purely as fuel and sleep as a necessary evil. It's been said that some highly driven corporate leaders speak of their bodies as if they were lithium batteries. With rapid technological advances that fuse us to our devices, it easy to see how we are becoming cyborgs. Human evolution could then be compared to system updates on our computer.[4]

Yet the more we push our bodies and the more stress becomes a way of life, we come to recognize that we are bodies that age, become ill, and eventually die. That message seems to get lost amid the always-on pace of our digital lives. We can create virtual selves that defy gravity, live vicariously through avatars, and program reality however we choose. Such freedom can be exhilarating. Though we may lose ourselves in an entire afternoon of digital stimulation and imagination, "we flesh-and-blood humans live back in the real world (and) have still aged four hours, missed lunch, denied ourselves bathroom breaks, and allowed our eyes to turn red."[5]

Perhaps the disconnect that many of us feel is that the more time we spend in our digital, programmed lives, the less we are in sync with nature and the circadian rhythms built into our analog bodies. The common experience of jet lag illustrates this, especially when we travel eastward across the Atlantic Ocean. "What we often forget is that our bodies are not quite as programmable as our schedules. While our technologies may be evolving as fast as we can imagine new ones, our bodies evolved over millennia, and in concert with forces and phenomena we barely understand. It's not simply that we need to give the body rhythms; we can't simply declare noon to be midnight and expect the body to conform to the new scheme."[6]

My sleep patterns certainly affirm this. Near the summer solstice the bright morning light wakes me up at 4:45 a.m., despite the shades in the room. I quickly put on a black face mask, which gives me some more precious sleep time. This is certainly not a problem near the winter solstice! In any case, amid my urban lifestyle I long for daily patterns and rhythms more connected to the cycles of the sun and moon. It may seem nostalgic, yet for all the bright digital clocks on the microwave, stove, and cable box, to name a few, I long to be more in sync with the deep wisdom in my body that flows from a circadian connection to nature. What that means, of course, is also coming to terms with an ever-changing body that ages,

4. Rushkoff, *Present Shock*, 95.
5. Ibid., 88.
6. Ibid., 92.

occasionally gets sick, and eventually dies. My question is this: Can going to church keep us mindful of these truths and integrate them into the sense of ultimate reality we encounter in worship?

Why Is Ash Wednesday So Popular?

I am always struck by the number of young adults who attend the Ash Wednesday service. Many of them I do not recognize and most do not attend regularly, but somehow they find something authentic in the visceral reminder of their human frailty. In a society that glorifies youth and sanitizes death, maybe there is a deep yearning for a tangible reminder that speaks the truth of mortality.

The liturgies of Ash Wednesday and the Three Days (from Maundy Thursday to Easter) hold the tension of death and life, mortality and resurrection. To be human is to experience not only blessing and gratitude, but suffering and finitude. Liturgical theologian Don Saliers names these two "requisites" of human existence that are linked to Christian worship: "a sense of wonderment and awe at the mystery of God becoming flesh, and an awareness of suffering and the interdependency of all things."[7] It is only through human struggle, hardship, death, and awareness of human injustice and the pathos of life that divine revelation can be known at all.[8] In Christian liturgy, the paschal mystery of Jesus' death and resurrection becomes the primary paradigm for a paradoxical spirituality that embraces death and life, emptiness and fullness, despair and hope.

When trying to explain the paschal mystery to a group of catechumens and seekers, I discovered that it was the example of nature that eventually struck the chord. We observe the dying of the earth each autumn and its rebirth in the spring. The vivid and breathtakingly beautiful red and orange autumn leaves never fail to move me deeply. In October, at least in many North American locales, nature is most stunning right before its yearly death, certainly a metaphor for human life as well. Yet in spring, as I write this, I am just as awed by buds gradually appearing on bare and seemingly lifeless trees. Lengthening days and warmer temperatures brings a rebirth of spring that signals hope even in the midst of insurmountable circumstances.

---

7. Saliers, *Worship as Theology*, 191.
8. Ibid., 192.

The community begins its paschal journey on Ash Wednesday, what liturgical theologian Ben Stewart calls a "small scale, ritualized, near death experience."[9] I was fascinated to learn that many Jews wear a white kittle on Yom Kippur. A kittle is a white burial shroud, a reminder that in death we are all equal. One rabbi said that on Yom Kippur you are preparing your body for death. You don't eat or drink or make love. It's like a near-death experience.

Even as Jews reflect on one's death as a means for spiritual renewal, for Christians Lent ushers in a season of reflection on baptism and preparation for the feast of resurrection. Though we come to terms with our own mortality and ashes are smeared on our foreheads, baptism leads to new life and resurrection.[10] Ash Wednesday presses "the earth back into our skin"[11] in an embodied ritual action; and the community is called, thereby, to acknowledge not only the fragility of human life, but the vulnerability of the earth itself.

All through the Three Days death and resurrection are juxtaposed. After all, we are not enacting a passion play; we are ritualizing the mystery of faith as reality for our lives today. The washing of feet on Maundy Thursday expresses the servanthood that flows from the baptismal call to live the paschal mystery in daily life. Though the ritual seems awkward for us today, I invite those present for this liturgy to consider the vulnerability that is asked of us: to allow our bodies to be touched, perhaps by a stranger. Through such ritual practices our bodies learn the heart of our faith: Christ's love poured out for the world.

Though some churches prefer to spiritualize the services of Holy Week, the ancient liturgies we inherit are embodied—analog, we might say. In the traditional Good Friday liturgy the cross is paradoxically acclaimed as a sign of resurrection. Worshippers come forward to offer a non-verbal sign of reverence to a symbol of vulnerability and loss. The Easter Vigil takes place not on a sunny spring morning but at night: "Even as we laud the candle, we know it burns in the midst of deep darkness . . . Even as we cry in joy at the immanent dawn, we cry out in the darkness of pain and catastrophe. In both senses, 'this is the night.'"[12] The Easter Vigil is the most embodied of all liturgies and filled with primal symbols of fire, darkness, light, water, oil, bread and wine. I continue to hear first-time Easter Vigil attendees describe how moving and transformative the liturgy was for them.

9. Stewart, "Ash Wednesday," 18.

10. Ibid., 18, 20.

11. Ibid., 23.

12. Farwell, *This Is the Night*, 9–10.

They often mention the multisensory experience of the vigil and how it encapsulates within one service the essence of the Christian faith.

In each Eucharist and during the liturgies of Ash Wednesday and the Three Days, the paschal mystery is celebrated ritually in community. Theologian Richard Gaillardetz writes that "it is in the life of a community of believers that we discover the graced character of daily living, and it is within the life of the community that we are schooled in the distinctive rhythms of paschal living."[13] In addition to seeing death and life in nature, we could say that human life also has a paschal character as we confront loss and vulnerability.

Aging and Disabled Bodies

The most common experience of vulnerability most of us will share is aging. It's not really a matter of whether, but rather when some kind of debilitation will occur. Everyone seems to face something a little different, depending on genetics or lifestyle.

Most of us would rather not talk about what lies underneath it all. Writer Tim Kreider says he will be first in line if they ever develop DNA rejuvenation or some other longevity technique. Then he adds, "But we don't have a choice. You are older at this moment than you've ever been before, and it's the youngest you are ever going to get. The mortality rate is holding at a scandalous 100 percent. Pretending death can be indefinitely evaded with hot yoga or a gluten-free diet or antioxidants or just by refusing to look is craven denial."[14]

When I think of the body's vulnerability, I always think of my mother's physical limitations as a result of polio she contracted when in high school. Though now nearly eighty, she still is able to travel and walk with the support of a walker, crutches, or battery-charged scooter. I remember my mother often encouraging me to be thankful for simple things like walking and running, as most of her life she's had limits on what could she could do physically. When I talk or write about honoring the body, I wonder the reaction of my mother and others who have had struggles with their bodies, perhaps even wishing they had a different one. Whether struggling with body image issues, a disability, aging, or confusion regarding gender identity, it is often difficult to come to terms with this intrinsic yet complex aspect of our identity.

13. Gaillardetz, *Transforming Our Days*, 77.
14. Kreider, "You Are Going to Die."

Phil Hefner, one of my former seminary professors, currently defines himself as mobility challenged; simply getting around is a daily chore. Though he writes of his own particularities, he believes "that living disabled is in some ways an epitome of being human—a pattern that we will all follow at some point in our lives, whether defined as disabled or not."[15] It was only in Hefner's late sixties that his severe back pain was diagnosed as spina bifida, though he had been aware of physical challenges throughout his life. He adds that those living with a disability are always aware of their dependency as simply moving about becomes a challenge. Hefner notes that to be an enfleshed human means that one of the ways the hiddenness of God is revealed is through our vulnerable bodies. In his state of being disabled, Hefner is able to say that "we meet God when we experience utter dependency."[16] Many of us do not want to be a burden to others as we face debilitating illness, yet Hefner's experience reveals the spiritual gifts of grace that are possible when we move toward acceptance of aging and mortality.

Being at Home in Our Bodies

Aging and disability are not the only bodily challenges. Many people struggle with body image in a culture that suggests that attractive bodies are those which are thin, toned, and young. Liturgical theologian Kimberly Bracken Long adds that "falling far short of those ubiquitous images of perfection, it seems that few of us revel in our bodies as magnificent gifts of a creative, creating God. Yet the revitalization of worship in many parts of the church depends, in part, on our reclaiming our bodiliness and rediscovering the embodied nature of our worship."[17]

Writing as a member of Generation X in 2000, Tom Beaudoin suggests that bodily piercing and tattoos are a response to the alienation young adults felt due to virtual realities, including cybersex and the threat of HIV in the 1990s. "These bodily incisions stay with us for the rest of our lives. They will be one certain source of continued identity amid the flux of identity in our simulational popular culture."[18] Beaudoin names these markings as the desire for spiritual experience that is embodied, and cautions that institutions that fail to acknowledge this generation's need for bodily,

15. Hefner et al, *Our Bodies Are Selves*, Kindle loc. 270.

16. Ibid., Kindle loc. 424.

17. Long, *Worshiping Body*, 22.

18. Beaudoin, *Virtual* Faith, 141.

religious-like branding will not be able to connect with them effectively.[19] Tracing a cross on a person's forehead—with oil at baptism and liturgies of healing, and with ashes on Ash Wednesday—is the best example of this kind of marking in worship.

Finally, to speak of the body is to acknowledge a plethora of experiences, contexts, attitudes, and body images. Theologian Nancy Eisland lived with a congenital bone defect and proposed a provocative theology of the "disabled God," connecting the image of body with disability, Eucharist, and community. She cautions that embodiment has an ambiguous character and warns against glamorizing the body. A eucharistic understanding of a disabled God—represented by the risen Christ still bearing the disabling wounds of crucifixion—must reject the image of the perfect body. "In the United States where a fetish for perfect bodies drives people to self-flagellation in overzealous exercise, to mutilation through plastic surgery, to disablement in eating disorders, and to warehousing and stigmatizing people with disabilities, young and old, the eucharistic message that affirms actually existing bodies is desperately needed and offers healing body practices."[20] Though the texts and physical actions of the liturgy may suggest reverence toward human bodies, it is equally important that in Sunday school and confirmation classes, for example, children and youth explore the implications of embodied spirituality for sexuality, body image, and overall stewardship of the body.

In a similar way theologians Andrea Bieler and Luise Schottroff take this even further by naming the diversity of bodies that come to the eucharistic table: pregnant women; those carrying cancer, HIV, and other illnesses; those struggling with eating disorders; those who have been raped and abused; those gendered as male, female, trans, or in between; those sexualized as gay or straight; those racialized as Black, White, Hispanic, or Asian. For all of us, our bodies are "constantly changing in inward condition and outward appearance . . . They are 'archeological sites' holding innumerable body memories of pleasure and ecstasy, illness and pain, as well as alienation."[21] All of these examples reveal the vulnerability of the body and the challenge of living fully as embodied human beings.

19. Ibid., 79–80.
20. Eiesland, *Disabled God*, 116.
21. Bieler and Schottroff, *Eucharist*, 133.

Funeral Practices

In a chapter on mortality and the body's impermanence, it is appropriate to add some thoughts on bodies at the end of our lives. There may be no area of congregational worship life more in need of careful theological reflection than funerals, particularly in White-dominant Protestant contexts. The dualism that was named earlier finds expression in memorial liturgies in which there is often no concern whether any bodily representation of the person is present or not. One of the primary reasons memorial services may be so popular could be the growing prevalence of cremation and the increased possibilities for arranging services that require no dealing with the body of the deceased. However, at the heart of the issue, it seems to me, is the belief for many North Americans that the body doesn't matter after death. "That's not really Grandma," we tell our children. "She has gone to live with Jesus." The body at death becomes a shell, something to be disposed of quickly and expediently. This is represented in this popular poem sometimes read at funerals:

> Do not stand at my grave and weep;
> I am not there, I do not sleep.
> I am a thousand winds that blow . . .
> Do not stand at my grave and cry;
> I am not there,
> I did not die.[22]

Moving as the poem may be to many people, such thinking is at odds with the importance of the body as named in Christian theology and liturgy. We may think about someone's personality and spirit, but it is their body that we imagine in our memory. And so it is in worship. The bodies of the faithful are washed in baptism. These bodies receive the laying on of hands at confirmation and anointing with oil in rites of healing. The body is honored in a multisensory liturgy that makes generous use of gesture and ritual. And most importantly, at the Eucharist the faithful share a bodily experience of a meal, eating and drinking. Therefore, at a memorial liturgy without a body—or the ashes of the deceased—present, I feel a great absence. I sense this loss most profoundly at the commendation rite at the end of the liturgy: "Into your hands, O merciful Savior, we commend your servant, Jane . . . Receive her into the arms of your mercy, into the blessed

22. Mary Elizabeth Frye, 1932.

rest of everlasting peace, and into the glorious company of the saints in light." To recite those words over air, so to speak, makes it seem like this is not an embodied person we are commending to God, but merely the memory of a person.

Theologian Thomas Long strongly challenges the disembodied Christian funerals that have become common today. He notes that if people believe that their most true self is a soul and not a body, the old-fashioned concept of needing a body at the service is unnecessary, costly, morbid, or even embarrassing to our practical and spiritual sensibilities.[23] Long acknowledges there are plenty of situations in which a body, coffin, or ashes cannot be present for a memorial liturgy and that Christians can certainly "raise the resurrection song," but questions this as the new norm. Despite a biblical anthropology that does not divide body and soul, Long wonders whether a body seems of lesser importance at a funeral because "we esteem the spirituality of the mind over the materialism of the body." Even though we talk about the body as a "shell," we go to great lengths to recover a body or even some of the remains when someone is lost at sea or crushed in the World Trade Center disaster, for example. By paying attention to these deep human responses to death, we might rethink why the presence of a body, or at least the ashes from cremation, should be present at a Christian funeral or memorial service.[24] Though a pastoral case for the presence of the body at worship goes against the grain of societal practice, I urge religious leaders to have these important conversations—not necessarily when a family has already decided what they want to do following the death of a loved one, but in less anxious contexts such as sermons, classes, and other congregational settings. For example, I would encourage a family to have the ashes of the deceased present at a funeral—perhaps along with photographs—to emphasize the importance of the body of their loved one.

Incarnation: Gift and Limits

A Christian spirituality is incarnational, embedded in the flesh-and-blood experience of being human—what I have been calling our analog lives. Perhaps these embodied connections are not being made in our new digital context. Yet, for me, this embodied analog reality is the heart of what we celebrate at Christmas when we speak of the Word made flesh, on Ash

23. Long, *Accompany Them with Singing*, 23.
24. Ibid., 33–34.

Wednesday when ashes are placed on our forehead, at Easter when we hear accounts of Jesus' risen body, and at funerals when we honor the body of the deceased. Though we give thanks for our bodies and how they are wonderfully made (Ps 139), in church we also confront our mortality and the limits of our bodily existence. In one way or another we will all face illness, aging, disability, and a wide array of contexts in which our bodies are a source of vulnerability, loss, and eventually death as we move through time. Our relationship to time itself, the theme of the next chapter, is also a worthy topic for reflection. In our analog lives nothing lasts forever, other than the promise of God to be faithful in both life and death.

SPIRITUAL PRACTICES

1. If you preach or compose prayers for worship, does the assembly hear mentioned and/or pray not only for those who are sick but also those living with disabilities, eating disorders, or various kinds of abuse? Consider ways that embodied worship helps people treasure the gift of the human body while acknowledging its vulnerabilities as well.

2. Consider the Buddhist practice of meditating on your own death. Listen and consider writing down some of the wisdom that comes to you for the living of your life now.

3. As more of our lives become digitized, can analog clocks or other items remind us of our mortality and the cyclical rhythms of life? Consider spiritual practices that connect you to the earth and its seasons. Decorate your worship space and home in ways that suggest not only the liturgical seasons, but also winter, spring, summer, and autumn. For example, bare branches in Advent can evoke a wintry landscape that also suggests themes of waiting and stillness.

4

24/7

Finding the Time

IT HAS CHANGED MY life. I'm not referring to a religion conversion. I'm talking about my personal relationship with my iPhone and the power and mystery of the Internet. For most of us, our devices are companions that accompany us 24/7. Can you even remember the time before Facebook, Twitter, 4G, iPhones, iPads, apps, Skype, and, of course, the cloud? How is our sense of time affected by the 24/7 realities of digital life? Can the concept of Sabbath be an antidote to lifestyles that have no time for reflection and spiritual renewal? Can corporate worship ground us in a different sense of time? Those are the questions for this chapter.

Let's begin with the ways we *love* our smartphones and laptops, our iEverythings and our eLives. They are awesome, magical, cool, fun, and constantly at our fingertips. We have become dependent on our devices and many of us rely on them 24/7. We can hear a song we like and an app will let us know the artist and title. We can then download it instantly on iTunes or listen to it on Spotify. Apps track our steps, give us directions, provide entertainment and news programs, take and edit photographs, and even store one's personal healthcare directives in the case of an emergency. I have a meditation app that goes with me everywhere I go, complete with soothing sounds of bells and gongs. If I remember a couple mere words from a book, song, poem, or well-known phrase and want to use it in a sermon, I can Google what I remember, and more times than not I come up with the exact source.

I must admit, though, that I have a love-hate relationship with technology. I am dazzled by everything that is at my fingertips instantly. Yet there are so many choices that I can read, listen to, download, and do online that it is sometimes overwhelming. I feel that all this techno-energy is with me 24/7 and, unless I make some conscious decision to unplug, shut my email program, or go for a walk without my phone, I'm never really away. Even downtime doesn't feel relaxing when I remain connected.

With all the time-saving devices invented in the past decades, you would think that we would be enjoying life, reveling in lives of leisure. Rather, we are busier than ever. Is there a connection between the 24/7 world in which most of now maneuver and our perception of time?

Consider this: the default answer these days for "How are you doing?" is "busy" or even "crazy busy." We brag about how busy we are. People in a number of occupations—including clergy—bemoan how long they have gone without a day off, sometimes finding their self-worth in a nonstop lifestyle. In a conversation with seminary students about our overly scheduled lives, an international student from Hungary was baffled by our country's workaholism. After observing her classmates for two years, she was troubled by the constant low-grade stress, competition, and drive that seem always present. Our compulsion to achieve and succeed at any cost means that many of us lack the needed rest and downtime that could bring some equilibrium to our lives.

Not Enough Time

The result of this busyness is that no one thinks they have enough time to do what they have to do, let alone time for leisure. Time has become a commodity we seek to manage and control. Most of us try to fit as much as we can into each day, often sacrificing sleep and activities that rejuvenate body and soul. Sociologist Judy Wajcman notes how Americans feel more rushed and harried than ever, while leisure time seems at a minimum. Yet, research shows that the average workday length and the amount of leisure time at our disposal have remained more or less constant over the past decades.[1] How is it that our supposedly time-saving devices make us feel as if we have less time? For one thing, since the industrial age and the increase of capitalism, time is seen as money, and therefore faster is always better and more lucrative. Time not spent earning money is wasted time.[2]

The title of a book by Douglas Rushkoff sheds more light: *Present Shock: When Everything Happens Now.* Rushkoff, a media theorist, contends that

1. Wajcman, *Pressed for Time*, 4–5.
2. Ibid., 16–17.

we are living in the future we have been waiting for. But no one has time for it. Though we sought an instantaneous network where time and space were compressed, it's not a Zen sense of the present moment that we are living. Everything is like a CNN news feed. "People meters" track our reactions to politicians or news before we even have a chance to think about them.[3] All of the notifications, alerts, social media updates, texts, and news flashes that are pushed to our smartphones intrude on our lives "with the urgency of a switchboard-era telephone operator breaking into a phone call with an emergency message from a relative, or a 1960s news anchor interrupting a television program with a special report about an assassination."[4]

This new sense of time can feel frenzied, making it harder for us to unwind and truly relax. Ben Eggers calls it "iTime," a reality in which there are no longer boundaries between public and private, day and night, work and leisure. "iTime oozes everywhere, driving out downtime."[5] Constant connectivity means that our work colleagues, family, and friends expect us to be always available and respond almost immediately to texts and emails. If we set boundaries and do not respond immediately, our inbox simply accumulates and we may later feel guilty that we have not responded to something important. For many of us, this sense of always being available leads to a manic compulsion, always needing to be online so we do not miss out on anything. Time itself is now mobile, portable, and "deeply compressed, weighing heavily on the person who has too much to do, not enough time to do it."[6]

When Downtime Is Boring

Even our leisure time is managed these days. We return from vacations needing rest and recovery. As much as we crave downtime, we have difficulty being idle. Most of us turn to digital devices in every spare moment. I find myself tempted to reach mindlessly for my phone in an elevator, on a bus, or sitting at a park bench. Gone are scenes of teenagers staring into space. There seems to be no downtime that is not filled with some digital activity or stimulation. Have you wondered what this does to our experience of time and to our ability to truly to be comfortable alone with nothing other than our own thoughts or our sensory appreciation of the natural world?

3. Rushkoff, *Present Shock*, 47.

4. Ibid., 79–80.

5. Agger, "iTime," 121.

6. Ibid., 124.

"Just keep busy!" That's what I remember being told as a young boy. If I entered one of my moody *funks*, as I now call them, my parents suggested the answer was to do something to take my mind off whatever I was feeling or concerned about. On the one hand, I think this is good advice. When feeling down, it is always good to go for a walk, call a friend, cook, or do something active. But on the other hand, I am less sure that simply being busy is the cure for some of the things that weigh on our hearts.

One colleague suggested that leisure not recognized as the gift that it is may be interpreted as boredom. We call this unstructured time boredom because we lack the imagination to take advantage of it. One thing that kids resist, whether decades ago or now, is boredom. A mother told me that she doesn't know how to get her teenage boy off his smartphone to read a book, cook, go outside, or do something creative. As an adult I still wonder who I am if I am not working, producing something, or making myself useful in some way. Yet I have come to appreciate that some of my most creative ideas have come out of times that seemed empty, if not boring. So I'm working on being comfortable with boredom and being open to learning from the absence that accompanies it. Sherry Turkle, a social scientist who specializes in studying the psychology of people's relationship with technology, suggests that boredom can be a gift that leads to creativity, imagination, and the ability to be at home with ourselves. It certainly is counterintuitive for us to consider boredom as positive.

Since boredom often lacks the stimulation of other people or activities, it may suggest loneliness. Yet, for Turkle, whereas loneliness suggests the absence of people, solitude brings us back to ourselves.[7] The more we become comfortable with who we are, the more we will bring a calm, steady presence to the challenges that come our way. For example, though time spent online is filled with a sense of urgency and constant stimulation, daydreaming opens us to new possibilities. "It helps us develop the base for a stable self and helps us come up with new solutions. To mentor for innovation we need to convince people to slow things down, let their minds wander, and take time alone."[8] Of course, putting any of this wisdom into practice means that we will need to exercise a sense of restraint, believing that keeping our email program closed some of the time or leaving our phone at home on a walk will have long-term benefits for our overall spiritual health.

7. Turkle, *Reclaiming Conversation*, 61.
8. Ibid., 77.

No Time for Church?

What does any of this have to do with church? Ideally, time set apart for worship should help us cultivate more reflective lives. Yet, when life seems overwhelming and there is little opportunity for rest and renewal, it is understandable that people choose to absent themselves from Sunday morning church. After all, it takes effort to get there. Some services are simply boring and irrelevant, sadly. Shopping, entertainment, and sports activities are readily available. Why not stay home and surf the Internet? Yet, these choices seduce us back into a manic sense of 24/7 time, tethered to commerce, constant stimulation, and the need to be productive, even in our leisure time.

Could it be that our constant activity and striving for achievement, success, and technological solutions to life's problems suggest that we lack the stance of receptivity needed to accept life as gift? Despite our lip service to the things of God, including the concept of grace, we live as if our identity is determined by our work, and the need to prove ourselves by what we accomplish. With no downtime for reflection and replenishment, is it even possible to be settled and at peace internally?

Josef Pieper, a renowned philosopher from the last century, challenged the pressing concerns of society that defined human worth solely in terms of work and achievement, manipulation, and control. When we lose sight of our role as created in the image of God and put ourselves at the center of the universe, he suggested, the sin of pride seriously threatens culture, and brings about despair and restlessness. Though written seventy years ago, Pieper's words seem as relevant today as ever. Pieper believes that leisure isn't simply a break that returns us to more work. Rather, work exists for the sake of leisure. To Pieper, leisure isn't merely what we think of as free time or hobbies; it is a spiritual attitude and, more concretely, practices such as silence, stillness, solitude, and contemplation. In other words, perhaps leisure is to simply be at home with our thoughts and feelings. In this sense, leisure's purpose is to make us more human and more aware of the reality of creation and life itself.

> Compared with the exclusive ideal of work as activity, leisure implies (in the first place) an attitude of non-activity, of inward calm, of silence; it means not being "busy," but letting things happen . . . For leisure is a receptive attitude of mind, a contemplative attitude, and it is not only the occasion but also the capacity for steeping oneself in the whole of creation . . . Furthermore there is a certain serenity in leisure. That serenity springs precisely from our inability to understand, from our recognition of the mysterious nature

of the universe; it springs from the courage of deep confidence, so that we are content to let things take their course.[9]

"What does this understanding of leisure have to do with worship?" you may be asking. Many people have viewed going to church as a moral imperative, making oneself pleasing to God, or to receive some tangible benefit, rather than something that opens our hearts to the gift of life itself. In a time marked by consumerism and instant gratification, words about solitude and inner reflection seem more needed than ever, yet ever more disconnected from the everyday rhythms and habits that actually shape us. Nevertheless, we see practices of meditation and mindfulness being introduced into business and work contexts. More and more people are turning to yoga and tai chi to provide a release from stress. Spiritual practices have become a way to provide some balance and respite in our fast-paced lives.

Worship as Spiritual Practice

In light of these cultural and technological realities, I propose that we hold up Sunday worship as the primary spiritual practice for Christians. There may be a tendency to think of spiritual practices in church as things like contemplative prayer and small groups, as well as other devotional, study, or service opportunities. Though these things can have great significance to some people, I am suggesting it is also important to make sure that the Sunday assembly is itself a spiritual experience, one central and orienting for both the community and the individuals within it. Worship will be most valued when it deepens the spiritual life and all that it means to be human. Yet, rather than focusing on the self alone, the fruits of liturgy will be ideally expressed in service, social justice, vocation, and commitment to the common good.

To put it differently: worship reminds us of another dimension of time and of what truly matters in life. Any such consideration needs to mention Abraham Joshua Heschel, one of the most significant Jewish theologians of the past century. To Heschel, industrial and technological advances have made us less aware of the both the beauty of creation and our common humanity. Rather than fixating on building, mastering, and conquering space, we should receive the gift of time represented by Sabbath observance. As Heschel writes, "There is a realm of time where the goal is not to have but to be, not to own but to give, not to control but to share, not to subdue but

---

9. Pieper, *Leisure*, 47.

to be in accord."[10] Sabbath practices have the power to shape how we live all the days of the week, sensitive to the needs both of the earth and other human beings. Heschel's work on Sabbath offers prophetic words not only for Jewish spirituality, but for all who find it hard to disconnect from the pull of technology. Sabbath—whether for a day, a week-long retreat, or even a few minutes of unplugging—is detachment from the gods of technology, and offers a paradoxical hope for human progress and development. This view of Sabbath demands not that we renounce technological civilization but that we are able to have a sense of independence from it. In regard to all external gifts in society, we learn how to have them and how to live without them. "On the Sabbath we live, as it were *independent of technical civilization:* we abstain primarily from any activity that aims at remaking or reshaping the things of space. Man's royal privilege to conquer nature is suspended on the seventh day."[11] A liturgy filled with ancient rituals and unplugged from distraction need not be boring and disconnected from contemporary life. Rather, worship as a spiritual practice can ground us in the present, provide meaning amid our restlessness, and bring us back to our identity as children of God.

Countercultural Celebration

In reading Heschel's words, you may be thinking of other kinds of gatherings that enable us to step out of our busy everyday lives: birthdays, holidays, sporting events, and parties, to name a few. These events certainly provide needed respite from our normal rhythms, yet do they form us to become more receptive and open to an alternate way of being in the world?

Josef Pieper roots true leisure in the celebration we know as worship, an occasion that affirms "the basic meaningfulness of the universe and oneness within it" as we step outside the confines of our otherwise stressful lives. Rest from work is thus always linked with divine worship, in which we find our true wealth apart from material abundance.[12] Though the idea may be counterintuitive, worship is not for the sake of something else, but an end in itself. In that sense liturgy is a priceless gift in which we are reminded of our identity and worth as human beings. Liturgy does not accomplish anything in the way we usually define accomplishment. Marva Dawn even once called it a

10. Heschel, *Sabbath*, 3.

11. Ibid., 28–29.

12. Pieper, *Leisure*, 48–51.

"royal waste of time."[13] Pieper speaks of divine worship in which we are lifted out of our everyday lives through the visibility of a sacramental participation, that is, connection to tangible reminders of God's presence in everyday life. We are thrown into ecstasy, transported from the weariness of our workday world into "an unending holiday" and the "heart of the universe."[14]

Such a view of worship is truly countercultural and will be difficult to sell in a world marked by advertising and consumerism. Understanding this, biblical scholar Walter Brueggemann goes even further by holding up the concept of Sabbath as an act of resistance. A way of life centered in Sabbath is rooted in our religious tradition and counters a lifestyle that reduces "all human life to the requirements of the market."[15] We live in a rat race that leaves us restless, longing for something more or different for our lives. As a tool to resist mere consumption and production, Bruegemann holds up these grace-filled Sabbath values:

> You do not have to do more.
> You do not have to sell more.
> You do not have to control more.
> You do not have to know more.
> You do not have to be younger or more beautiful.
> You do not have to score more.[16]

Sabbath, in all the above examples, could be read simply as time apart for Sunday worship, or an intentional period of time (a day or more) for rest and renewal, ideally disconnected from technology so that there is space and time for a different focus than the 24/7 feed usually before our eyes.

We could learn something from the Jewish Sabbath Manifesto that encourages not only a yearly Day of Unplugging but also a weekly time-out to embrace these principles:

a. Avoid technology.

b. Connect with loved ones.

c. Nurture your health.

d. Get outside.

---

13. Dawn, *Royal Waste of Time*, 1.
14. Pieper, *Leisure*, 73–74.
15. Brueggemann, *Sabbath as Resistance*, x.
16. Ibid., 40.

e. Avoid commerce.

f. Light candles.

g. Drink wine.

h. Eat bread.

i. Find silence.

j. Give back.[17]

For Christians, weekly worship reminds us of these important values, and our communal participation encourages us to carve out countercultural, intentional time for true rest, rejuvenation, and spiritual renewal.

To be countercultural as suggested above doesn't mean escaping the world. The question is not whether to spend money or to use technology, but to seek balance. Albert Borgmann, who specializes in the philosophy of technology, speaks of the "device paradigm" in which gadgets, devices, and other mechanisms are turned into commodities that rob us of our essential humanity. He proposes "focal practices" that help us engage the larger world and things of ultimate concern.[18] Focal practices could include things like reading, playing musical instruments, cooking, dining, walking, sports activities, arts, fishing, gardening, and endless other activities that connect us to our bodies, and often to the earth. Roman Catholic theologian Richard Gaillardetz, using the work of Borgmann, proposes that "our principal difficulty is not technology itself but our inability to differentiate between the central life practices that we wish to preserve because they bring meaning and grace and those spheres of life for which efficiency and cost-benefit analysis ought to reign."[19] For me, sacramental worship is the spiritual practice that has the potential to remind us to live richer, fuller, more embodied lives in the world. When one Episcopal priest was asked why worship was important to him, he replied that he needed to be reminded of his true identity and calling, and of what is utmost importance in his life.

Time as Gift

In other words, worship is a focal practice that can help direct our attention to the things that truly matter. And there are other practices that can

17. http://www.sabbathmanifesto.org.

18. Borgmann, *Technology and the Character of Contemporary Life*, 196–209.

19. Gaillardetz, *Transforming Our Days*, 44.

so guide us. While many of us turn to our smartphones or computers in any spare moment, we could all do well to make sure we take time to get outside, spend time with loved ones, and find some time to simply think, reflect, and be. Robert Farrar Capon said that a human's "real work is to look at the things of the world and to love them for what they are."[20]

When we have a gadget in our hands we have a world of endless digital options to stimulate and distract us. Is there anything that can help us to see the natural beauty right in front of our eyes? Gathering together for worship and engaging in spiritual practices can help us refocus our lives. Simply paying attention is the spiritual work of a lifetime.

As I have suggested throughout this chapter, rather than our seeing time as a commodity, being in church together can help us to see it as pure gift. I remember this offertory prayer from an earlier Lutheran worship book: "we offer you what you have first given us: ourselves, our *time*, and our possessions, signs of your gracious love."[21] Maybe we need to change our language and stop talking about managing time, fighting time, trying to save time. Maybe we are the ones who need saving. It's not that hard work and excellence, using our gifts, and making a difference in the world aren't important. But in the end, we have nothing we need to prove. Our work may be our calling, and even a source of deep joy, yet our worth does not depend on working sixty or seventy hours a week. Lutheran theology insists that we are not saved by good works. Let's take the "s" off that last word: we are not saved by good work either.

So how does this work for people like me—a religious professional whose work is to lead worship? Isn't it ironic that those who talk most about grace are sometimes the ones who find it hard to live it? When leading worship is part of our work as well, even if it is renewing for us, it isn't really time away. Religious professionals will need to carve out other opportunities for downtime. If our vocation is all about calling people to a balance of work and rest in their lives, how important it is for us to model such a commitment ourselves.

Dorothy Bass says busy people think they need more open slots on their calendar, but soon those slots fill up as well. Surely time is more than a 24/7 sense of one thing after another. What we need, Bass says, is "time of a different quality. We need the kind of time measured in a yearly round of fasts and feasts, in a life span that begins with a newborn placed in her

20. Capon, *Supper of the Lamb*, 19.
21. *Lutheran Book of Worship*, 66.

parents' arms, and in a day that ends and begins anew as a line of darkness creeps across the edge of the earth."[22] When I think of my experience of time, I love our sacred calendar that is connected to cycles of the sun and moon, the hours of the day, a variety of seasons that echo our human story and context.

My sincere hope is that going to church for worship teaches us week by week to receive time as a gift. After all, we are formed by these words in the Great Thanksgiving: "it is our duty and joy in all times and places to give you thanks and praise." We've lost the ancient sense of 24/6 + 1. Time for rest and renewal, whether in the liturgy or in intentional times of Sabbath, teaches us to let go of the need to be in control and to trust not only in God but in a mystery at the heart of time itself.

> Whatever is foreseen in joy
> Must be lived out from day to day.
> Vision held open in the dark
> By our ten thousand days of work.
> Harvest will fill the barns; for that
> The hand must ache, the face must sweat.
>
> And yet no leaf or grain is filled
> By work of ours; the field is filled
> And left to grace. That we may reap,
> Great work is done while we're asleep.
> When we work well, a Sabbath mood
> Rests on our day, and finds it good.[23]

If worship teaches us the sanctity of time and the importance of Sabbath rest, it also opens our eyes to beauty—the theme of the next chapter.

22. Bass, *Receiving the Day*, 3.
23. Berry, "Whatever Is Foreseen in Joy," 20.

SPIRITUAL PRACTICES

1. If you agree in principle with the need for intentional times of unplugging and Sabbath, but find it nearly impossible to do so, develop a rule of life that outlines specific spiritual commitments.[24]

2. Be intentional about keeping your email app or Web browser closed for portions of the day (even if you are doing something else on your computer); turn off the *push* function on your smartphone so you do not constantly receive notifications; spend time in nature or with other people without your laptop or smartphone.

3. Try to model a countercultural approach to time. Ideas could include: 1) avoid complaining about being busy and instead learn how to say "no" to certain invitations and engagements; 2) block out time for time off from work and/or renewal on your calendar; 3) if you are a religious leader, begin to see Sabbath time as essential to your ministry and as important as what you define as work.

---

24. Vryhof, *Living Intentionally: Creating a Personal Rule of Life.*

5

Design

Seeking Beauty

WHEN MY BROTHER URGED me to purchase my first Apple product, he mentioned how sleek and beautiful these products were. "A delight to hold in your hands," he would say. Since my first Apple computer, I have also enjoyed using an iPod, an iPad, and an iPhone, and can testify to not only what amazing things these products can do, but also what they look and feel like.

The designers of Apple products recognize the human yearning for aesthetics. Even the packaging is intended to be as pleasing as the product inside. The appearance of the device itself seems as important as the actual functioning of the computer or phone. The various applications, backdrops, and accessories are designed to respond to our every mood and whim. No wonder people are drawn to their iPhones with almost religious devotion. Indeed, these devices serve many more functions than what they were ostensibly designed to do.

We may respond to the design of our smartphones and agree that they are cool. But are they beautiful? How do we experience beauty? Can it be mediated to us via screens? Is a beautiful sunrise on the Internet equal to experiencing an actual one outdoors? Is there a difference between listening to music with earphones and attending a live concert? Are we able to be moved by various kinds of media in the same way that people in former eras were stirred by the natural creation?

In this chapter I will consider the role of beauty in our lives. I will explore how aesthetics may affect our reaction to certain musical or ritual elements in worship. Finally, I will look at the role of beauty in our experience of being human and how its presence in liturgy has the potential for transformation—not only of us, but of the world. We may speak of a beautiful picture, a beautiful song, a beautiful day. We know the popular line, "Beauty is in the eye of the beholder." Does that mean that our response to beauty is completely subjective? Is it all a matter of personal taste?

Let's first briefly consider aesthetics. Frank Burch Brown, who writes on theology and the arts, notes that "while aesthetics was initially tied to the notion of a science of sensory knowledge and taste, it soon came to be understood more broadly as theoretical reflection on matters pertaining to the arts, beauty, and whatever else attracts attention by virtue of formal, sensory, and expressive qualities."[1] Within the realm of theology there is an increased consensus that religion and art share a common purpose. Therefore, aesthetic experience must be considered when speaking of liturgy even if questions of style and taste make the task difficult. While worship is rooted in aesthetically rich forms—music, metaphor, ritual, image, architecture—it doesn't mean that everything "aesthetic is especially religious or that everything religious is especially aesthetic."[2]

I also think of beauty more broadly. The search for earthly beauty is part of the human experience. Who can remain unmoved by hearing Annie Lennox sing of a "thousand beautiful things," or Louis Armstrong sing "what a wonderful world"? John O'Donahue, known for his writing on the topic of beauty, suggests that "the human soul is hungry for beauty" and that we are "most alive in the presence of the Beautiful."[3] We often confuse glamor with beauty, yet the truly Beautiful offers us an "invitation to order, coherence, and unity. When these needs are met, the soul feels at home in the world."[4] Though beauty is not limited to the realm of religion, I claim that we experience the beauty of God through all that it means to be human, most especially through our bodies and sensory organs.

What about beauty and church? How often do you link those two concepts together? Would you use the word *beauty* to describe your experience of worship? Do you seek beauty in your life, and in particular, in your encounters with God? Or do you resist such language, believing that there are more important ways to speak of spirituality? Whatever your reaction, let us consider the role of beauty in human experience and in worship.

1. Brown, "Aesthetics," 14.
2. Ibid., 14.
3. O'Donahue, *Beauty*, 2.
4. Ibid., 5.

There are many reasons people might choose whether to attend church or not, yet I doubt that the presence or absence of beauty is one of the reasons that would be named. I am going to suggest that experiencing beauty is a deep human need, and that the beauty in worship helps us step out of our ordinary lives to immerse ourselves in an experience of ritual, art, and music that connects us to the divine before we return to our everyday lives. Certainly worship is not the only context in which we encounter beauty, but our experience of the liturgy can train us—open us—to behold the beauty of God in all times and places.

My love for designing, planning, and leading worship has an innate aesthetic sensibility to it. It is as natural to me as a love for football or history is to someone else. I loved playing church as a boy. My mother sewed simple altar hangings for me in the correct liturgical colors. Sometimes I would create church layouts using Legos. I would actually design worship bulletins for fictitious churches. Later I began to notice the disproportionate number of gay men in the fields of fashion, art, dance, music, and, yes, liturgy. Their aesthetic might be one reason that property values go up when gay people move into a new neighborhood. Designing liturgy that is moving and inspiring is important to me, and I believe that a worship service that is beautiful has the power to touch the edge of mystery even while connecting us to our common humanity.

Delight in God's Beauty

There is no lack of strategies to help churches grow. I have certainly come up with my own list: Make sure preaching is relevant. Speak to the spiritual hungers of people today. Bring a sense of excellence to everything, whether the church website, bulletin, or the building's feeling of hospitality. Finally, making worship beautiful is also on my list, but I do not hear much about it from others. I wonder if one reason many of our churches are empty is that too many services are uninspiring and the worship spaces unattractive. These flat experiences lack an authentic sense of sacred space and time. Are we more concerned with speaking to people's minds rather than creating multisensory experiences of beauty that are moving and have the capacity to lift us out of our everyday lives? Though I can read the script of a play, listen to a recording of a symphony, or view a piece of art online, there is something powerful about attending a live artistic event.

Let's think more concretely about beauty in worship. The psalmist speaks of a deep desire for beauty: "One thing I ask of the Lord; one thing I seek: that I may dwell in the house of the Lord all the days of my life; to gaze upon the beauty of the Lord and to seek God in the temple" (Ps 27:4). Many of us sing the hymn "Beautiful Savior." We speak of the beauty of the heavenly realm. Yet, I wonder if Protestants are shy about admitting that we encounter the beauty of God in our own "temples" when we gather for worship.

For Orthodox Christians, participating in the divine liturgy is described as heaven on earth. Yet as Orthodox theologian Alexander Schmemann writes, beauty is never necessary, functional, or useful. Those who love God do not simply discuss the meaning of faith, they "represent it in art and beauty." For example, the presider vested in a beautiful chasuble can be seen as wrapped in the glory of God. "In the Eucharist, we are standing in the presence of God, and like Moses before God, we are to be covered with his glory."[5] Like Schmemann, Rabi'a, an eighth-century Sufi mystic, also described worshipping God simply for its own sake and as a way to experience God's beauty: "O my Lord, / if I worship you / from fear of hell, burn me in hell. / If I worship you / from hope of Paradise, bar me from its gates. / But if I worship you/ for yourself alone, grant me then the beauty of your Face."[6]

Several years ago, my congregation participated in a discernment process to clarify what should be the focus of its time and resources in the next several years. The process, not guided or directed by me, included many opportunities for the congregation both to listen to one another and to share their own observations, hopes, and dreams. Worship is not mentioned explicitly in the purpose statement that was the outcome of the process, but the words *mystery* and *beauty* appear. After a broad, inclusive gathering of data, here's what the task force proposed:

> Purpose Statement: *Open to the Mystery . . . Connect, Strengthen, Serve with Joy!*

> Guiding Principles:
> - *Act with courage.*
> - *Be radically inclusive.*
> - *Cultivate empowering relationships.*
> - *Delight in God's beauty.*
> - *Engage with intention.*

5. Schmemann, *For the Life of the World*, 29–30.
6. Rabi'a, "O My Lord, If I Worship You."

Many of these values correspond well to numerous progressive faith communities, but I love that "Delight in God's beauty" also appears. For many, the liturgy is an experience of God's beauty. Whether in the ancient rituals and vestments, the bodily senses and gestures, or the entire flow of the service, there is a deep connection to God as mystery. Worship sets us apart from purely social service ministries, as valuable and essential as they are. Worship forms us for service in the world.

To understand what the many young adults in our community were responding to in worship, a number of years ago we prepared a questionnaire. We hoped to learn whether or not the form or style of worship might be part of their aesthetic experience. A majority agreed with the statement that they are drawn to traditional liturgy because of its beauty and because it moves them. There were consistent, strong negative responses to contemporary worship and music. This may come as a surprise to older church folks who assume all young people want praise bands and MTV-style projected images. The millennials in my congregation named a certain depth of meaning possible within traditional hymn texts. The majority sensed that liturgy can convey the range of human emotion and be an avenue to the transcendent. That being said, I always offer this disclaimer: millennials in urban Chicago or in my congregation may respond differently than their counterparts in other places; but at the same time we dare not say that no young adults are drawn to traditional, liturgical worship.

Some of the millennials I encounter describe having a checklist when they church shop. Others talk about having a strong, immediate, and intuitive sense when they find their new church home. Folks easily name things like welcome, diversity, music, and preaching as being what draws them. But I wonder about something harder to fit on a checklist: an encounter with beauty or the transcendent, and how that moves people and connects with their longing for God.

If, as the Orthodox say, worship is heaven on earth, we can release creative energy in enacting artful liturgy. We can join with liturgical theologian Joyce Zimmerman and "implement ritual so rich that bodily emotions are unleashed, then create the silent space for the bodily emotions to be suspended so poetic transposition can happen."[7] In that sense, we might evaluate the artistic nature of liturgy not by what kind of music is chosen, but by whether the experience touches us on a deep and emotional level.

7. Zimmerman, "Beauty and the Beast," 30.

Beauty and Being Human

Throughout human history and in all cultures, art has been the medium to express the depth of human experience. When I was studying music education in college, my choral director talked about the power of music to connect us with human emotion. He spoke about tension and release in music and how that corresponds to the experience of life itself. The arts have the power to move us, open our hearts to wonder, and also to express the depths of agony and despair.

Sometimes you hear someone say that they only come to church for the music. No doubt some folks struggle with saying the creeds and question whether their beliefs are truly orthodox. Yet they can be moved by music and art—something deeper than the purely rational that they trust most often in their lives. Theologian Richard Viledasau asks whether an unorthodox kind of faith can be stirred in one who responds to the emotion in Bach's choral music, for example, while not espousing traditional belief. Apart from questions of assent to doctrine, he posits the possibility that great religious music, even in the face of death, can evoke "in the hearer a belief in the beautiful, a belief in life . . . raising thereby the question of the grounds of belief."[8] If we are all responding to the same deep mystery at the heart of human life, perhaps we need to also validate those who are less willing to use religious language yet are nonetheless moved by the power of the arts to express beauty and the depth of the human experience. This may be another instance of Tillich's definition of God as whatever is of ultimate concern to us.

Yet art is rarely mentioned these days as an important gift of the church, despite Martin Luther's insistence that next to the word of God, music is one of the world's great treasures. One Roman Catholic priest laments that we are willing to take stands for the sake of freedom, justice, and peace, but not for beauty and the arts—all of which are celebrated in the liturgy. Lutheran theologian Joseph Sittler called liturgy the "supreme record of all that gladdens and saddens and maddens human beings."[9] Beauty is a basic human need, not a luxury able to be purchased only by the rich. In fact, poor and oppressed people are often the ones who can demonstrate true celebration in a genuine care for beauty and the arts, and what it means to truly mark an important occasion.[10] The loving devotion

8. Viladesau, *Theology and the Arts*, 45.

9. Hovda, *Amen Corner*, 214.

10. Ibid., 215–16.

invested in a Hispanic congregation's celebration of Our Lady of Guadalupe is one example of this.

Though we experience beauty in worship, terror is also a part of the human experience. Liturgical theologian Don Saliers speaks of the stunned silence that can envelop us we experience either the surprising wonder of beauty or the senseless agony of something traumatic. Terror and beauty are usually unacknowledged until tragedy strikes or we are drawn into the mystery and splendor of the *other*.[11] Ritual—particularly the Eucharist—is an uncommon occasion in which these two central aspects of human experience are held in tension. We sing the glory of the cross, for example, and proclaim that the Crucified One reigns. For Saliers, when grief and hope are bound together there is a "liberation back to our full humanity." As speech arises out of silence, perhaps we are able to behold beauty only after we have witnessed deeply human experiences of terror, agony, loss, or grief.

Liturgy and Preaching as Art

One of the things I love about the design of worship is that it is a kind of convergence of liturgy, art, ritual, theology, and spirituality. In employing all our senses, worship affirms the goodness of creation and the incarnational reality of embodiment. Embodied worship is a far cry from viewing the Holy Spirit as simply dwelling in our hearts. Rather, through materiality mystery is named in sacred space and time, ever inviting us to see the world with new eyes. French philosopher, mystic, and activist Simone Weil writes that "there is, as it were, an incarnation of God in the world, and it is indicated by beauty. The beautiful is the experimental proof that the incarnation is possible. Hence all art of the highest order is religious in essence."[12]

Many Protestants agree that we employ the arts in worship. Let us consider, however, that liturgy *itself* is art. Homiletics professor Charles Rice uses the incarnation to speak of the embodied word made present not only in art and liturgy, but in preaching. Believing that preaching itself is art, Rice contends that "we must recognize our common reliance upon metaphor and appreciate the artists' gift for showing us, in their inimitable ways, what is important in human life on earth."[13] Both artist and preacher are asked to tolerate and express ambiguity, even while expressing the inex-

11. Saliers, "Beauty and Terror," 205, 302.

12. Weil, *Simone Weil Reader*, 52.

13. Rice, *Embodied Word*, 95.

pressible, relying on both discipline and imagination for this creative task.[14]
Rice asserts that although churches have drifted into business models for
ministry, the church is more than a patron of the arts. The church plays the
artist because it lives by imagination, expressing itself most fully through
story, symbol, drama, music, and ritual. In other words, it relies on "material expression of what is deeply known but is difficult to say."[15]

The design of a homily or sermon should not only involve rhetorical
skill and delight the listener, it should also use artistic examples such as personal experience, literature, film, items in the news, and local occurrences
to deepen the message. These provide "examples of the unnoticed presence
of the transcendent dimension—at least as a question—in every aspect of
human life . . . the beauty of this message itself, although not necessarily the
primary content of preaching, is implicitly present in its correlation with
our transcendent desire and need for God."[16]

Both art and liturgy are ultimately concerned with more than creating
positive feelings. Rather, they give insight into our ordinary lives, even as
they invite growth and change. Encountering the same piece of art will differ
on each occasion, and the same is true for the liturgy each time it is enact-
ed.[17] This variety is particularly true when observing the church year and its
various festivals. Our experience of the season of Advent or the liturgy of
Christmas Eve, for example, will vary from year to year, based on the context
of our lives and the events in the world. Even when texts and hymns remain
constant, the meanings and experience vary from one occasion to another.
For example, receiving ashes may be more poignant after receiving a cancer
diagnosis, or Advent may be especially resonant if a couple is pregnant.

To see liturgy as art is not equivalent to simply admiring sacred music,
but instead is "congruent with the self-giving of God in our humanity at full
stretch . . . If the art of liturgical assembly is to be revelatory, it must seek
the whole emotional range: from the ecstatic praise to the depths of lam-
entation, and the ordinary, daily struggle of being human."[18] Art not only
expresses the full range of human emotion, but also its yearnings and even
its questions. Even if the liturgy lacked music, poetry, and fluid movement,
it would still quality as art. For "when we are about the things that matter

14. Ibid., 96.

15. Ibid., 101.

16. Ibid., 214–15.

17. Empereur, "Is Liturgy an Art Form?," 107.

18. Saliers, *Worship as Theology*, 198–99.

most to human beings—enhancing our environment, passing on to others what we have found most important, making sense of our experiences, expressing our deepest feelings of truth and beauty, or simply doing the work of daily living—we are not far from what is signified by the word *art*."[19]

Creativity and Beauty

All the stirring words mentioned so far about worship and art do not negate the fact that sometimes worship is anything but inspiring and beautiful. As mentioned earlier, there is great subjectivity regarding preference in music or other stylistic elements. We are not all moved by the same things. Some suggest that quality and excellence are the issues here. These are certainly factors, but I may not respond emotionally to a certain type of music, regardless of how well it is performed. The subjectivity of such responses leads me and other worship planners to make sure that the music planned in worship will have a blend of simple and complex melodies and familiar and new tunes. In any given liturgy, I hope that there will be some musical or ritual element that each person will find meaningful in some way.

There is great diversity of style, form, and content in our artistic creations—all reflecting delightful elements of imagination and innovation in the human spirit. The twelfth-century Christian mystic Hildegard of Bingen suggests that human creativity springs forth from the wonder of creation: "God created humankind so that humankind might cultivate the earthly and thereby create the heavenly." How important it is, then, that congregations draw out the creativity of artists, musicians, dancers, and poets, to name just a few. Whether those preparing the worship space, vocalists and instrumentalists rehearsing, or others decorating the church for a feast or liturgical season, beauty is created not only to give glory to God, but also to inspire the assembly that gathers. Think of God as a creative Spirit and the source of our gifts as well, as this wonderful hymn text puts it:

> Come to us, creative Spirit,
> in this holy house;
> ev'ry human talent hallow,
> hidden skills arouse,
> that within your earthly temple,
> wise and simple, may rejoice.

19. Rice, *Embodied Word*, 97.

Poet, painter, music-maker,
all your treasures bring;
craftsman, actor, graceful dancer,
make your offering;
join your hands in celebration:
let creation shout and sing!

Word from God eternal springing,
fill our minds, we pray;
and in all artistic vision
give integrity:
may the flame within us burning
kindle yearning day by day.

In all places and forever
glory be expressed
to the Son, with God the Father
and the Spirit blest:
in our worship and our living
keep us striving for the best.[20]

Community of the Beautiful

Though we might first locate beauty in nature or art, we dare not forget that human beings are created in the image of God, and thus are themselves beautiful. Alejandro Garcia-Rivera, a Hispanic theologian steeped in liberation theology, locates beauty within the human community. When the words of the Magnificat are fulfilled—the lowly lifted up and the hungry filled with good things—the "community of the beautiful" is created.[21] That is why liturgist Nathan Mitchell describes worship as a choice in which we reeducate our desire. Our worlds are too small, and the things we desire too self-centered. In liturgy, however, we align ourselves with the beautiful work God does for us, and then we open our hearts and hands to the vulnerable and the needy. "The rituals of public worship discipline desire by teaching how to pay attention—how to pay attention to that Beauty whose

20. David Mowbray, "Come to Us, Creative Spirit" (Hope, 1979).
21. Garcia-Rivera, *Community of the Beautiful*, vii.

67

being, Aquinas said, 'flows forth to enliven all things.' Simply stated, worship is desire in a state of supreme attention."[22]

"The world will be saved by beauty," Doestoevsky famously said.[23] For our purposes, we can wonder if it can be saved apart from people gathering to worship. No doubt there are many motives to make the world a better place. Yet, perhaps an encounter with beauty is most needed when the world looks bleak and its problems overwhelming. Joyce Zimmerman makes a bold claim and stunning proposal that artful liturgy has the potential to transform the world and bring about the reign of God. Though many elements done to "the very best of the assembly's ability" are important, what is more essential is that we "strive (dare) to approach the mystery of divine presence and in the presence we are transformed." In that sense, artful liturgy is literally "life-threatening, for in our surrender to the ineffable attraction of divine beauty we lose ourselves—die to self—so that we might be a new life beyond that which even our wild images could muster."[24]

Certainly, as I noted in the introduction to this chapter, we will be dazzled by the design of sleek gadgets and technological wizardry. They reflect the unique human spirit of creativity and ingenuity of these times. But unlike Christian liturgy, they do not invite us to die to self and to be born to a new and better life. At the same time, worship reminds us to treasure this life now: the natural beauty of creation, the human body, and the arts. This liturgical design gives meaning to our human experience of joy and suffering and forms us into a beautiful people of gratitude and praise.

And since *mystery* is a word that aptly describes God and evokes the beauty of life and death, we are ready to move to a topic deeper than words.

---

22. Mitchell, "Being Good and Being Beautiful," 554.

23. Doestoevsky, *Idiot*, 80.

24. Zimmerman, "Beauty and the Beast," 30.

SPIRITUAL PRACTICES

1. Study the ELCA's *Principles for Worship*, especially the sections on music and worship space.[25] Discuss the role of beauty in your congregation's worship life. How might those who design and plan worship in your community use a variety of arts to express the beauty of God?

2. If you project worship texts in your worship services, consider ways that images could be used during a reading, sermon, or time of reflection.

3. Lectio divina is a method of meditating on a Scripture passage. Find creative ways to also meditate on music, art, poetry, or nature as well.

25. *Principles for Worship*, 23–46, 67–96.

6

Access

Welcoming Mystery

"ALL ARE WELCOME." THIS phrase seems to be on nearly all church signs and websites. For years I have been saying these words—or something similar—each Sunday: "Whoever you are, whatever your spiritual journey, whatever the color of your skin, whomever you love or marry, and whatever you think of organized religion, you are welcome here. We hope that you will leave with a deeper sense of purpose and commitment to live your life with integrity and service in the world."

When I wonder whether longtime members or I will tire of such repetition, I continue to be surprised how such a simple welcome has deeply affected newcomers to the community—and continues to be important to regular worshipers. Apparently plenty of folks have not felt welcome in church. They may not be sure what they believe or how they fit in, or they have been wounded or angered by religion. When I recently mentioned this matter to a group of new members, and said welcome and hospitality were simply part of a message of grace and not that unusual, one man said, "You haven't been visiting other churches recently, have you?"

This chapter is going to consider the theme of access: first as it is expressed in the church's welcome and hospitality to strangers and those on the margins, then how digital access may affect our current religious and spiritual milieu. Finally, I will consider how a welcome to the *other* corresponds to openness to mystery in our lives.

Was I Welcome Or Not?

I feel lucky that I have always felt welcome in church and have loved worshipping each week throughout my life. My gifts, interests, and passions have been well received in the congregations in which I have served. I was elected to the church council and was involved in musical and worship roles already in my teens. During those years I had a wonderful pastor and mentor, Eugene Larson, who inspired and encouraged me to use my gifts in service to God. There was no doubt in my mind that I wanted to become a pastor.

Yet life is never simple. After years of struggle, by age twenty-one I accepted that I was gay. Five years later, while in seminary, I also felt a deep call to be in a loving, committed relationship with someone—in my case, a male seminarian. Taking our commitment seriously, we exchanged vows at a liturgy of holy union in 1987, many years before gay blessings—let alone gay marriages—were fashionable or normative. Being in ministry and being in a relationship were both non-negotiable to me, but only one of them could be fully public until 2009, when the Evangelical Lutheran Church in America changed its policies regarding the ordination of partnered gay and lesbian rostered leaders.

From my internship in 1986 through my first three congregational calls, I was fortunate to have colleagues, bishops, and parishioners who were quietly supportive of my decision to honor both ordained ministry and a committed relationship, even though I was not in compliance with official church policy. I was the "other" that countless national and regional church assemblies debated for years—as surreal and painful as that was for me. To live with the inner contradiction, I equated my relationship with a marriage, though officially I was not welcome in my own denomination to serve as a pastor. It was a bit like living in two worlds. I often had to change pronouns depending on to whom I was talking. For some, I would say, "*I* am going on vacation," and to others I would say, "*We* were leaving on Friday." In some ways it was a small sacrifice to make, and by and large I was grateful beyond words that I had access to both ministry and a significant relationship. Other gay and lesbian colleagues took different approaches and refused to compromise and came fully out of the closet, and usually were forced to leave the ministry. Still others found themselves in less safe settings and were removed from the roster when their relationships were discovered.

When I think back over the past twenty-five years, I can hardly grasp the social movement that I have lived through, leading eventually to a change in Evangelical Lutheran Church in America policy and the Supreme

Court legalizing gay marriage in 2014. Throughout those years, one could say that we were dealing with questions of access. Did the LGBTQ community have access—rights—to such things as ordination and marriage? Were we welcome to be fully ourselves not only in church but also in the workplace and the public sphere? How did the gospel—the good news of God's grace in Christ—help us respond to questions of welcome and acceptance?

The various welcoming movements in churches were inspiring to more than simply those affected by the reality of sexual orientation or gender identity. During the past eighteen years, I have continually heard how the message of welcome and inclusion has had a deep impact on straight newcomers and members. They want to be part of a community that is welcoming to all. They desire to raise their children in a church that values diversity and openness. And though they have not used theological concepts in conversations with me, it seems that the message that most resonates with them is God's unconditional acceptance, which we Christians name as "grace," "gospel," and "good news." Yet, even as many are seeking connections to a welcoming congregation, others are simply finished with organized religion. They are now sometimes referred to as "the dones." When we consider the theme of access, is there any connection between the demographic changes going on in churches and the new digital realities in our lives?

Digital Access

Elizabeth Drescher, who writes about issues of spirituality and religion today, uses the term *digital Reformation* to describe the intersection between recent technological advances and church. Drescher names not only digital technology but the many other societal changes that have occurred at a rapid pace since the end of World War II. She uses the word *access* to describe the new global reality in which we participate, co-create, and redefine authority, as well as ways the church can be revitalized by the digital context that now defines our lives. Whereas in previous church reforms religious professionals interpreted theological insights for the laity, Drescher notes that the Internet allows ordinary people today to have "access to technological means of connection, creativity, and collaboration with those resources that remained in the hands of a narrow elite even after the Protestant Reformations."[1] Theoretical and practical insights on theological, spiritual, biblical, and ecclesial themes are readily available on the Internet.

1. Drescher, *Tweet If You ♥ Jesus*, Kindle loc. 219.

Professional clergy are no longer seen as the sole experts on these topics. Whereas we have more options than ever to nurture a spiritual approach to life, many churches operate as if nothing has changed in the past fifty years. Thus it seems as if the "Church is just not living where the people are."[2]

Seminary president David Lose describes the digital pluralism that marks our time. The unparalleled access we have to information—including values and convictions that shape our spiritual lives—"exceeds what we can possibly process, creating an overload or super-saturation of information of nearly unimaginable proportions."[3] I know this to be true as I explore the dizzying plethora of news and entertainment that I can access in an instant online. When we consider the ambivalence of younger folks to jumping right into church membership and participation, though they may share our affinities with mystery or a sense of God in their lives, "they are not interested in simply receiving what feels to them like a prefabricated religious identity."[4] What they trust is their own experience and what they learn through conversation and statements from trusted entertainment figures, not to mention Facebook and Twitter posts. The church, in general, and religious leaders, in particular, no longer represent authority as they once did.

Whether we inside the church like it or not, this is the new normal. What does this mean for doing church in new ways? As we sometimes say about our congregation, "This is not your parents' church." Our experience with many millennials has brought some insights, along with plenty of new questions and challenges. Whether I see the glass as half empty or half full varies, I have to admit. Yet, let us continue to explore themes of access and welcome, and gifts that I believe can be found in this unique time.

Welcoming the Other: Bricolage

Most of the so-called welcoming churches value diversity and are quick to announce their openness to people of different backgrounds, races, sexual orientations, gender identities, religions, and socioeconomic statuses. To that list my congregation intentionally adds openness to those questioning and struggling with organized religion, whom I described above. The identities of individual worshippers are less fixed than they were previously. If I asked my parents if they are spiritual, they may not know what to say; Lutheran is

2. Ibid., Kindle loc. 3093.

3. Lose, *Preaching at the Crossroads*, 87.

4. Ibid., 90.

the label that defines them. But things are different with younger generations and, I have to admit, even with me. *Bricolage* is a delectably fun, exotic word that describes an eclectic mix of things. A number of scholars use bricolage to describe the individualism inherent in today's religious and spiritual marketplace, referring to a strategy of blending and mixing various elements to create something new. Diana Butler Bass argues that Christianity arose from a weaving of the "spiritual experience of Jesus, rabbinic Judaism, Greek philosophy, Gnosticism, and Roman paganism."[5] To Bass, many people have valid reasons for rejecting parts of their tradition while supplementing them with other experiences, and this approach signals the end of an outdated, irrelevant, or legalistic kind of religion. In its place "people are engaging in religious bricolage; they are 'doing it themselves,' as they pick up fragments of practice from various sources at hand and construct new sorts of Christianity, Judaism, Islam, and other religions."[6]

I am a Lutheran pastor but have my own bricolage. I go to Benedictine monasteries for retreats and am considering becoming a Benedictine oblate. I practice yoga in which there are Hindu chants. I meditate and value insights from Buddhism. I am nourished by perspectives and practices from a variety of Christian and other spiritual traditions. I have to also admit that a part of me is agnostic, particularly as I compare my Christian theology to that which the media portrays—since their portrayal is linked with the religious right and the accompanying values of certainty and exclusion.

Bricolage seems to be the reality of the day. One scholar worries, though, that "a careful sociological listening to contemporary voices reveals a trend toward the more general sacralization of the self."[7] Without the correctives of a community and the wisdom embedded in a religious tradition, we are merely picking and choosing spiritual elements that feel right to us. Taken to an extreme, we become our own god. In this case, the spiritual marketplace and individual bricolages reveal deficits in contemporary culture. Like so many things in life, there is something to observe and learn in both perspectives represented above. But let's take a look at how worship itself is changing and becoming more diverse.

---

5. Bass, *Christianity After Religion*, 151.

6. Ibid., 150.

7. Lyon, *Jesus in Disneyland*, 18.

Worship Bricolage

The selection of hymns and songs in recent hymnals represents a kind of bricolage drawing from different historical periods, styles of music, ethnicities, parts of the world, and denominational backgrounds. Since the 1980s it is a given that when I attend a special seminary or denominational liturgy there will be hymns and liturgical music that in some way reflect such diversity. There may be a Lutheran chorale, a Hispanic kyrie, a psalm with a Black gospel feel, and an ancient chant in the same service. In fact, some communities focused on outreach to young adults use the term *ancient-new* to describe a liturgy that blends multisensory elements from Christian tradition—candles, incense, icons—with contemporary innovations such as the use of projection screens and more contemporary music, for example.

In my congregation the Sunday morning liturgy itself is a kind of bricolage. As our basis we use *Evangelical Lutheran Worship*, yet additional hymns and liturgical texts supplement those in the hymnal. We ring a meditation bell—from Eastern traditions—as a call to silence and centering. Icons throughout the worship space include not only well-known traditional saints such as Mary, Mary Magdalene, and Francis of Assisi, but also J. S. Bach, Martin Luther King Jr., Dietrich Bonhoeffer, and even Ghandi.

When welcoming greater diversity in worship, a local faith community becomes connected to the wider global, catholic church. For example, it seems that most of the marriages in my congregation involve a Roman Catholic and a Lutheran or other Protestant. Our liturgy has elements that enable both partners to feel at home. Even the icon of Mary in the chancel is important in this regard. A Lutheran World Federation statement on worship and culture that has been widely discussed in liturgical circles and in recent publications over the past twenty years states, "First, [worship] is *transcultural*, the same substance for everyone everywhere, beyond culture. Second, it is *contextual*, varying according to the local situation (both nature and culture). Third, it is *counter-cultural*, challenging what is contrary to the Gospel in a given culture. Fourth, it is *cross-cultural*, making possible sharing between local cultures.[8]" This fourfold designation of worship (transcultural, contextual, counter-cultural, and cross-cultural) is its own kind of bricolage, and names the importance of welcoming elements beyond the local context. In our connections to other times, places, and peoples, in a sense we are accessing a God who is always more than we

8. *Christian Worship*, 24.

can imagine. Considering the space beyond our imagination offers a good segue to explore how mystery fits into all of this.

Welcome Mystery

For Christians, the incarnation of Jesus means that access to God is gained through that which is most human, or as we could put it, our bodiliness and the materiality of life. That is why sacraments remain integral as the means of grace to point us to the divine revealed in the stuff of everyday life. My spirituality is firmly rooted in all of these things. Yet, taken to an extreme, it is possible to be seen as implying that we predominantly find God in that which is familiar, such as our own setting, context, or experience. These are things and places that we know well and access easily.

On the other hand, in a world marked by globalization, digitization, and an emphasis on the theoretical and cerebral, to name God as mystery is liberating for me. Otherwise, God is simply a human projection of what we know and experience, and leads to sureness rather than openness. Many authors are distinguishing between *belief*, defined as assent to particular doctrines, and *faith*, defined more specifically as trust. When religion is about absolutes and certainty—in the form of beliefs—there is no room for doubt. My religious upbringing certainly left no room for questioning. When I went to college I felt I had all the answers to life, and they were found in the Bible. What a rude awakening it was when my first college course—Bible 101—debunked so much of the literalism on which my faith had been built. My four years of college involved a gradual movement from seeing all of life as black and white to seeing rich hues of gray. At the same time, I was struggling with my sexual orientation and clearly that added great complication. How could I reconcile what I knew to be most true about myself with a religious tradition that left no room for a meaningful same-gender relationship of intimacy and integrity? Such questions led to deeper biblical and theological inquiry in search of answers. Yet at the same time, I began to treasure mystery—living the questions rather than always having the answers. Since that time, I have loved these words by Rainer Maria Rilke from his *Letters to a Young Poet*:

> Have patience with everything that is unsolved in your heart and try to love the *questions themselves* as if they were locked rooms or books written in a very foreign language. Don't search for the answers, which could not be given to you now, because you would not be able to live them. And the point is, to live everything. *Live*

the questions now. Perhaps then, someday in the future, you will gradually, without even noticing it, live your way into the answer.[9]

With the above Rilke quote in mind, we can ask: Can churches be places that welcome questions? Can they be safe places for doubters, skeptics, and seekers? Can pastors be comfortable with not being able to answer every question, but simply let some be? Are we able to value faith more than certainty and hold up mystery as an antidote to theological systems that are rigid and closed rather than open to the *other*? In fact, can we begin to name God as *other* and reflect on ways that we welcome the mystery and all that is unknown to us, not only in God, but in other people and in the universe? The implications are many, from welcoming strangers in our country and in our congregation to welcoming that within ourselves that is less familiar or even scary. *How can welcoming the* other *lead to spiritual growth not only as a church but as individuals?*

I love a piece that spiritual writer Richard Rohr did for the NPR series *This I Believe.* He titled it "Utterly Humbled by Mystery." In it he reveals what he has learned throughout his lifetime. Though many religious people speak of having the answers, Rohr is comfortable with ambiguity. He hesitates whenever he is tempted to say "only" or "always." He finds it ironic that scientists can speak of principles of uncertainty while exploring a hypothesis, yet most of us relish "closure, resolution and clarity," which Rohr believes are the very opposite of faith. Rather, those who have met the holy are humbled by mystery, able to admit what they do not know. "They are in awe before the abyss of it all, in wonder at eternity and depth, and a Love, which is incomprehensible to the mind. It is a litmus test for authentic God experience, and is—quite sadly—absent from much of our religious conversation today. My belief and comfort is in the depths of Mystery, which should be the very task of religion."[10]

Welcoming Newcomers

Maybe welcoming mystery is a key to welcoming newcomers to our congregations. After all, guests are strangers and many of them today do not fit our previous assumptions about potential church members. Benedictine spirituality talks about welcoming strangers as if we were welcoming

---

9. Rilke, *Letters to a Young Poet*, 14–15.

10. Rohr, "Utterly Humbled by Mystery," para. 3–6.

Christ. Could church people begin to welcome newcomers unconditionally regardless of whether it leads to their belonging or even believing as we do? Can seekers and church shoppers who drop into our churches perceive a sense of openness, authenticity, and even mystery in the ways we preach, conduct the liturgy, and encounter strangers?

Jessicah Duckworth, a young theologian who has focused on these questions, suggests that the presence of newcomers is unsettling because the fluidity and liminality that defines their lives disturbs what we often consider to be "settled, determined, and fixed."[11] Duckworth goes so far as to say that the church will be saved through its relationship with these somewhat mysterious folks dropping into our churches these days.[12] By listening to their questions rather than giving pat answers, we take seriously their context and the human condition of "suffering, pain, loss, angst, horror, grief, and shame." In that sense, we walk together the way of the cross, and the dying and rising that is part of human life.[13]

Without the presence of newcomers, our congregations may die as they focus on themselves rather than strangers, the world, and God. "At the same time, these newcomer strangers lurk threateningly, representing by their presence a hope for a new community that requires the death of the old . . . Welcoming the Other and the stranger molds and shapes who we are and who we are to become."[14]

Access Is Not Just about Membership

On any given Sunday, my congregation's worshipping assembly is made up of longtime and newer members—about half of them millennials—and several dozen more young adults who are not members of the congregation. Some have been attending a few times, off and on, consistently for months or even years, but have never signed a worship registration card or made themselves known. When I do eventually get to know some of these newcomers, they often tell me that they appreciated the anonymity and the freedom to be present at first on their terms, without a sense of obligation.

This situation may be one snapshot of the future in which public worship in some contexts is a fluid gathering both of active members that

11. Duckworth, *Wide Welcome*, 35.

12. Ibid., 37.

13. Ibid., 101.

14. Ibid., 108.

support a congregation financially and assume various service and leadership roles and of those who hunger for community and spiritual connection but are suspicious of things institutional—such as membership and stewardship programs. David Lose wonders if the decline in religious participation is largely due to a generational shift in which younger people have multiple ways to consider what is important in their lives, are less likely to attend things that do not seem worth their time or effort, and are more likely to engage in activities that will make a noticeable difference in the world. Congregations that still talk about membership, pledges, and friendship pads, for example, may find that millennials may not respond to such language.[15]

It is possible to be a public church that welcomes people at whatever level of commitment they find themselves, while encouraging those comfortable with it to become more involved in the life and mission of the community. Sometimes I feel I am a pastor to two tracks of people: those open to being known and becoming members, and those simply dropping in from time to time—and to be honest, all kinds of variations on these themes. The default setting for most congregations is to welcome and get to know new people, and then invite them—in fact, expect them—to become members. Yet, as I have noted, that strategy does not work for a number of people today. I suspect that the larger the worship attendance, the easier it is for folks to slip in and out of worship without being invited to coffee hour or cornered to teach Sunday school or sing in the choir. It is often smaller worshipping communities that, usually with good intention, risk suffocating newcomers by being overly friendly at first. Based on my conversations with millennials, many do not return to some congregations because they either appear too needy or they give the impression that they are desperate for newer or younger members.

It is no doubt difficult for pastors and staff members to maneuver within a public church made up of both members and others in various levels of attendance, interest, or commitment. I am often torn between the institutional side of me, which is concerned with offerings, attendance, and having enough people to maintain the ministry of the congregation, and the other side, which wants folks to feel at ease getting to know the community and participate at whatever level is comfortable for them. My intuition tells me that in my current context it is probably better to err on the side of giving people space, in contrast to my earlier pastoral model of courting

15. Lose, "Emboldening Thought," para. 1–2.

someone and inviting them for coffee and conversation after they attend worship three or four times. On the other hand, the latter approach is the right one for those comfortable with church and eager to make connections with the pastor and a new congregation. Most of the time I am trying to read the signs and signals given to me by newcomers, later realizing that at times I should have followed up sooner or that in other cases my invitations made someone withdraw. Since I can never really know, I simply do the best I can and entrust the rest to grace.

As custodians of an institution, we need members who participate, contribute financially, volunteer, and assume leadership in our faith communities. Clearly, I believe we need to continue to invite people to become members of our congregations, conduct stewardship appeals, develop community, and provide opportunities for folks to grow in faith and commitment. At the same time, I continue to struggle with how to integrate those who may consider our communities their church home but not necessarily under the terms and conditions we set. If our only invitation is to a new member class, a certain percentage may never respond or, if pushed too strongly, may stop attending. If an invitation to a membership event may limit the number of people who respond, calling the gathering an introduction—or something similar—may allow such a session to appeal to both those on a membership track and those whom we might consider seekers or inquirers.

For those drawn to a deeper spiritual process of exploration and renewal, the catechumenate[16] may be a welcome alternative to membership classes. In my congregation, we call this catechumenal process Life Together and announce that it is designed for those who:

- did not grow up Christian and/or have not been baptized;

- are new to Lutheranism, liturgy, or a sacramental tradition;

- have been estranged from the church but are now drawn to community and communal worship;

- are sensing a stirring of the Spirit, yet filled with questions;

- may have grown up Lutheran but didn't think about it when they were confirmed, and would like to learn more about Christian faith and life in community;

- are parents wanting to grow in their faith as part of the baptismal promises they make on behalf of their children.

16. See http://catechumenate.org/index.php?page=about-us.

The catechumenate is meant to be adapted to each local congregational context and there are many resources available to assist with this.[17] To adopt a catechumenal method to overall spiritual formation for newcomers, consider this question: Rather than merely teaching people what Christians believe and describing the uniqueness of a particular congregation, what if our goal was to first get to know newcomers and seekers, hear their stories and questions, and discover what they are searching for?

Still Others, Still More

The ways we welcome strangers and newcomers, and the openness we have to mystery and not having all the answers, will lead us to encounter new and surprising people in our unique contexts, both as individuals and as faith communities. Another group of important outsiders that I would like to name briefly is people of other religious traditions. Interreligious engagement is happening more frequently in many places, and this encounter with strangers has the opportunity to not only expand our horizons but also deepen our own faith commitments. In some cases we may consider important social issues such as immigration, and in other situations congregations may explore creative ways to get to know people of other faiths. A wonderful resource for this is *Engaging Others, Knowing Ourselves: A Lutheran Calling in a Multi-Religious World*. In it Mark Swanson, a professor of Christian-Muslim studies and interfaith relations, notes that mutual hospitality is challenging, particularly when people of privilege become guests, and when this hospitality "puts us in places where we are not in control, were we do not know what will happen next, where we need to be taught how to behave, where we depend on others for our well-being."[18]

As we consider themes of access and welcome, there is always more. There are always more outsiders and people on the margins, not only to welcome, but also to honor as beloved children of God. Our encounter with mystery means that God is always more as well. The Holy Spirit continues to open our minds and hearts in fresh, creative, and sometimes unfathomable ways. The welcome we proclaim in baptism is more radical than we ever imagined. The welcome may be clear, but are our churches making connections with the people in our pews? That is the topic for the next chapter.

---

17. Bushkovsky et al., eds., *Go Make Disciples* is an excellent ecumenical guide.
18. Swanson, "New Realities," 39.

SPIRITUAL PRACTICES

1. Does the worship service in your congregation invite a sense of mystery? Invite pastors, staff, and members to discuss this question.

2. Consider how your individual journey is a bricolage. In what ways is your congregation's worship a bricolage? Are you able to welcome practices from other traditions while retaining your own identity within a particular religious tradition?

3. When you greet newcomers are you first imagining what they would like to know about you or the congregation, or are you asking questions to get to know them? Consider how welcoming newcomers—and any kind of *other* in our lives—can be a rich spiritual practice.

7

Connectivity

Embracing Real Life

THINK OF THE WAYS you are connected to the Internet and how you use so-cial media. When reaching a new destination—a hotel, a conference center, a host's home—usually one of the first things we do is get the password for the wireless network so that we can be online. When not connected in that way, we may begin to feel out of sorts and even anxious.

Though we use the word *connectivity* to describe the reality above, I believe the heart of spirituality is *connection*, not only with God, but also with self, others, and the world. In other words, the very thing that defines what it means to be human. My question is this: Is our online connectiv-ity superseding moments of unplugged reflection and our human need for connection to God, the earth, and face-to-face contact with others?

This chapter begins with a story about my reflective teenaged persona. From there I will consider the digital connectivity that is part of our every-day lives. I will then make the case that church can be a place to connect not only with God, but also with what it means to be human. Preachers, as reflectors in residence, have the unique and challenging task of making such connections.

Reflections and Connections

I first began writing journal entries when I was thirteen. I certainly felt connected to God as a child—not only in church, but also in the Colorado mountains and in the beauty of music. Yet in my early teens my introspective side began to blossom, and I began to reflect more deliberately on questions of faith and life. This nerdy reality both horrifies and delights me when I think back to it. Since I didn't have male friends with whom I could relate, I began to share thoughts and feelings with several girls. This, of course, created confusion for at least one of them, as it seemed like such emotional intimacy also signaled romantic interest. It would take nearly eight more years for me to straighten that all out in my mind and heart.

One of these "girlfriends" and I used the word *pithy* to describe our personal sharing. We believed that our conversations were deep, significant, and expressive. Like most adolescents, we were trying to become more comfortable in our skin and in the world, and as much as we found a soulmate in our connection with each other, we also wondered whether we were over-analyzing, and at times we wished life could be simpler, as it seemed to be for our classmates. Of course, now I know that everyone was struggling in some way.

Journal writing was a way for me to express my experience of being human at that time in my life. Already then, I sensed that life was full of both great joy and struggle. Because my faith was formed by Lutheranism and a strong dose of fundamentalism, I cringe at some of the language I used in my writing then. Yet, I also realize that my reflective side was beginning to express the paradox that marks what it means to be human—that life is beautiful beyond words and also filled with loneliness, loss, and heartache. Since music was also an intrinsic part of my life, I would write songs to express what I considered inexpressible.

As I grew older, I began to consider this reflective side a great gift. The flip side of this introspection, however, is also my greatest challenge. My self-awareness brings a sensitive connection to the struggles of others and has been a significant source of my being able to preach out of the human condition we all share. At the same time, a side effect can be melancholy and a fixation on discerning the meaning of life that sometimes inhibits living a rich, adventurous life. The older I get, the more I realize that each of us holds such a paradox. Something in each of us is a gift for the world but is often coupled with an opposite challenge, usually marked by some vulnerability. This paradox becomes the spiritual agenda for our personal growth.

Constant Connection

Of course, in our fast-paced lives today, I wonder if any of us has time for reflection anymore. Canadian writer Michael Harris distinguishes between time before and after the Internet. Born in 1980, he is among those who can remember what he calls "a time of absence," marked by things like day-dreaming and being alone with your thoughts. Like Harris, I catch myself idly reaching for my smartphone in a spare moment and realize there is no such thing as free time anymore if you carry a device that is always competing for your attention. Harris writes that future generations will not even be able to conceive what being alone with one's thoughts means. He grieves that we have pretty much lost this aspect of life forever because of our constant state of connectivity. In fact, he describes the new reality as the end of absence, or what he calls "the lack of lack."

Harris's experience with the demands and stress of constant connec-tivity led him to take a month-long sabbatical from the Internet, Twitter, Facebook, texting, and, yes, his computer and mobile phone. He called it his "Analog August."[1] During this time he admits to dreaming of email and going through withdrawal symptoms. When he seeks an epiphany at the end of the thirty-one days of disconnection, all he can say is, "I was so ir-revocably, damnably, utterly wired to the promise of connection that I have to constantly, every hour of every day, choose *which* connections matter in a given moment." When he realizes how exhausting this new challenge will be, he also says "how very worth it" it will be as well.[2] It is a spiritual choice, really, like others that we continue to make throughout our lives.

Like other writers, Harris fears that what we lose with constant con-nectivity is the ability to experience solitude, or as I am naming it, the ca-pacity for reflection. He mentions Thoreau going to the woods not due to loneliness, but to enjoy the company of his true self. Harris then quotes the well-known line by Thoreau that many of us have loved over the years:

> I went to the woods because I wished to live deliberately, to front only the essential facts of life, and see if I could not learn what it had to teach, and not, when I came to die, discover that I had not lived.[3]

1. Harris, *End of Absence*, 189.
2. Ibid., 187.
3. Thoreau, *Walden*, 85.

Yet Harris goes on to name a less famous line in which Thoreau adds, "I did not wish to live what was not life, living is so dear."[4] In our time, we must discern what is real life and what is not. Removing himself completely from society was not an option for Thoreau. Neither is going back in time and deleting the reality of the Internet in our lives. It is essential to note here that technology itself is neither good nor evil. "The most we can say about it is this: *It has come.* Casting judgments on the technologies themselves is like casting judgment on a bowl of tapioca pudding." The question is: How will we live now? What choices will we make?[5]

The technological advances of the past decade have come at such lightening speed that we are still adjusting to them. I often wonder whose task it is in society to help us achieve a healthy relationship to our devices while urging caution when they separate us from our authentic and life-giving relationships with one another, our bodies, and the earth. Harris concludes his book by observing that absence is not going to return to our lives naturally. "Just as we decide to limit our intake of the sugars and fats that we're designed to hoard, we now must decide to sometimes keep at bay the connectivity we're hardwired to adore."[6] For many people there is no downside to the amazing technological advancements of the past decade. I believe, however, that, like many things in life, we need to have a nuanced view of technology, not only noting its wonders and enticements, but its dangers as well.

This challenge is a matter of discernment. For me, it raises questions of what it means to be human and what connections ultimately define us. Perhaps those of us who remember a different quality of life before constant connectivity can be wise elders enabling such reflection, not with a wistful desire to go back in time, but by opening up conversations about a needed balance in our lives. Historian Noga Arikha believes that since she remembers a time before everything was digitized, it gives her an opportunity to relate wisely to technology. She grieves the reduction of "three-dimensionality to the flat screen . . . Where has slowness gone, and tranquility, solitude, quiet? The world I took for granted as a child, and which my childhood books beautifully represented, jerks with the brand-new world of artificial glare . . . faster, louder unrelated to nature."[7]

4. Ibid.
5. Ibid., 197–200.
6. Ibid., 206.
7. Arikha, "Internet and the Loss of Tranquility," 42.

For a number of years, writer Nicholas Carr has been asking us to consider what makes us human and whether our constant connectivity threatens any of those essential things. As we experience "more of our lives through disembodied symbols flickering across our screens," we risk losing our humanness, and "sacrifice the very qualities that separate us from our screens."[8] Carr writes those words following a chapter in which he considers the work and thought of Joseph Weizenbaum, computer scientist at MIT, after he designed a well-known computer program named ELIZA in the 1960s. Weizenbaum expressed ambivalence about technology making important decisions for human beings in the future since computers lack the human qualities of compassion and wisdom. He urges us to refuse to delegate to computers tasks that demand wisdom.[9]

Religion Must Begin with the Human

What kind of theological anthropology can assist us as we maneuver through the new digital realities of our lives? What separates us from machines? What makes us truly human? What is most at risk when we become more like our devices and they become more like us? There are difficult questions. If we begin not with questions about the nature of God, but with what it means to be a human person, we find ourselves in the realm of theological anthropology. According to Stephen J. Duffy, "theological anthropology explores the destiny of the human person and its resources and limitations in quest of that destiny."[10] For Roman Catholic theologian Karl Rahner, theology must take into account the contemporary situation, "which does not allow Christianity to appear as something indisputable and to be taken for granted."[11] Rahner is known for the "anthropological turn," in which—simply put—theology begins not with discussion about God, but about human experience.

Sometimes I wonder if many sermons and religious teachings today are so centered on God that they fail to help people make connections with their own lives and what it means to be human. As much as religious leaders would like to provide answers and tell people what we think they need in their lives, a more humble stance would be to listen, hear their stories, and learn what is on their minds and hearts these days, including

8. Carr, *Shallows*, 207.

9. Ibid., 207–8.

10. Duffy, *Dynamics of Grace*, 11.

11. Rahner, *Foundations of Christian Faith*, 5.

their perceptions of organized religion. In that sense, though pastors, and preachers in particular, are taught to exegete Scripture to find its meaning for today, we need to equally exegete contemporary society in order to hear the yearnings and needs facing people these days. In other words, unless we make these important connections with people, our words may be irrelevant and fall on deaf ears. Sometimes it may be a matter of making more connections with daily life. For example, once a colleague used the image of a selfie to speak of both Jesus and us as God's beloved on Baptism of Our Lord Sunday. During a heated election season when "The system is rigged" was heard often, I used those same words as a mantra, making connections with both the Scriptures and the contemporary context.

A Spiritual Revolution?

Many leaders of religious institutions lament the decline in attendance, commitment, and stewardship in churches today and seek creative and fresh ways to woo people to our congregations. Others are noting the spiritual revolution going on all around us. Some writers are even suggesting that we are living through a unique time of spiritual renewal five hundred years after the Reformation. What polls and studies continue to reveal is that Americans by and large still believe in God, pray, and have spiritual experiences. What is changing, though, is that many people today are finding meaningful connections with God, or participating in renewing spiritual practices, outside of traditional religious structures. While I am not sure many of the religiously unaffiliated would be able to articulate what they find missing in churches and synagogues, they are quick to name that they have experienced religion as exclusive, judgmental, and boring.

Writer Diana Butler Bass goes deeper with her analysis. Bass believes we are in the midst of a spiritual revolution in which the primary questions regarding the relationship between God and the world are changing. In past centuries, beliefs were of ultimate concern. The central religious questions had to do with the nature of God, how to be saved and attain eternal life, and how to be a good or moral person. The purpose of religion was to be a kind of mediator between the sacred and the secular. But today people are asking where God can be found in this world and how the divine presence informs their actions in everyday life. Most of Christianity, for example, has used what Bass calls "vertical language" to describe God. God's holiness is removed from the world and thus is found up in heaven, in sacred places, and religious rituals. Ancient texts, liturgies and hymns suggest a God in heaven who comes down to bring salvation to an unworthy people marked by sin and a world stained by immorality.[12]

Though I quibble with some of Bass's analysis and can point out preachers and hymn texts that offer exceptions to her generalization, I agree that we need to listen openly to people and their experience of church. Bass claims that she and many others are now experiencing and using horizontal language to suggest divine nearness. For example, she says that for her, "God, the spirit of wonder, or Jesus—it is often hard to label exactly—shows up in prayer; while walking on paths, hiking in the desert, or sitting in the sunshine; in the animals that cross my way; and in my dreams."[13] Bass goes on to describe how people are grounded in new ways today—grounded in the earth, the events of everyday life, working for a better world, and in God. Many of them consider themselves spiritual but not religious and have either been wounded by the institutional church or see it as broken and hypocritical. Bass makes the point that people still believe in God and have spiritual experiences, but we are in the midst of a spiritual revolution in which people are claiming personal agency in religion as they are in other aspects of their lives. By taking responsibility for their own spiritual lives, people are crafting a new kind of theology. A common thread seems to be a "God who is far more personal and close at hand than once imagined."[14]

I find much wisdom in Bass's analysis and take into consideration these realities when considering parish ministry, preaching, and spirituality today. Yet, her most indicting words are the ones that follow. She notes that many of the so-called nones are experiencing rich spiritual lives, while those within the church are always quick to point out the dangers of individualism and defend the importance of religious and civic institutions. Bass believes that the experience of millions of Americans is downplayed when these terms are used to describe them and their practices: "cafeteria religion," "navel-gazing spirituality," and "moral therapeutic deism."[15]

I appreciate Bass's strong warning to religious leaders to listen carefully to the experiences of others. At the same time, I believe that a community provides an important counterbalance to an individualism that can be overly centered on the self. For those of us who still believe church has

12. Bass, *Grounded*, 10–12.
13. Ibid., 12.
14. Ibid., 21.
15. Ibid., 22.

something to offer contemporary society, what can we learn from Bass's diagnosis? Bass believes the church is sleeping through the spiritual revolution—in other words, the connections are not being made. Even those of us in the institutional church, like me, who are deeply committed to spiritual renewal in our congregations, need to ask whether we are helping to make new and appropriate spiritual connections for people or whether we are repeating the same formulas, doctrinal explanations, and theological language from decades, if not centuries ago.

Despite her strong critique of the church, Bass nonetheless believes congregations are the most natural place for people to learn not only to recognize God's presence but also to be signs of justice and healing in the world. Interestingly, her challenge and invitation are for those within organized religion and those outside it. To me, her words below get at the gist of what it means to be human:

> It is surprisingly easy to join in: get off the elevator, feel your feet on the ground, take a walk or hike, plant a garden, clean up a watershed, act on behalf of the earth, find your roots, honor your family and home, love your neighbors as yourself, and live the Golden Rule as you engage the commons. Pay attention. Play. Sing new songs, recite poetry, write new prayers and liturgies, learn sacred texts, make friends with those of other faiths, celebrate the cycles of the seasons, and embrace ancient wisdom. Weep with those who mourn. Listen for the whisper of God everywhere. Work for justice. Know that your life is in communion with all life.[16]

Why wouldn't our faith communities be committed to such things?

Making the Connections in Preaching

For churches that use a traditional liturgical format, connections with everyday life can certainly occur in the intercessions, announcements, and contemporary hymn texts, but preaching is the primary place where they can be made. No doubt there are people in our congregations who appreciate sermons that explain scriptural texts or theological concepts, yet my experience is that too often sermons are essays on abstract topics rather than proclamation that connects with people's everyday lives. In addition, whether I am in the pulpit or in the pew, it seems that regardless of content or approach, people begin to drift after ten minutes or so. I believe that

16. Ibid., 284.

more times than not, in our fast-paced society, most of us preachers have sermons that are too long and too cerebral. Over and over I come back to the maxim: less is more. Many of the sermons I hear would be more effective if they were trimmed by about one third.

It's a strange thing to say, but I also feel that most sermons are too religious. Now hear me out. What I mean is that there is too much talk about the Scripture text, God, or some belief or religious practice, and too little connection with the hearer's everyday life. In other words, the connections are not being made for most folks. The topic may be of great interest to the preacher, but it can feel irrelevant to the concerns that our parishioners are carrying on any given Sunday. At the same time, some parishioners tell me that in some churches there are many stories from everyday life, often in a folksy style, but with little wisdom from Scripture or theology.

If preachers are reflectors in residence, then it is important to find the right balance between types of material in sermons. When I work with seminarians, I distinguish between what I call A and B content. B content is the heady stuff that preachers like: discussion of the text, God talk, and general theological or intellectual material. A little B content goes along way in an oral presentation, particularly with today's short attention spans. Unless the text is extremely controversial, such as Jesus' strong words about divorce or lopping off of limbs when our hands sin, my sense is that most folks are not primarily looking for a sermon to explain the Bible. Instead, they are hoping for connections with their lives in the world. Jesus knew the distinction. We could call Jesus' parables A content; they use material from ordinary, everyday life. Here is what I try to draw on for A material:

- examples and stories from everyday life;
- popular culture (movies, television, novels);
- events in the news;
- acknowledgement of the stress, worries, and pain people are carrying;
- literature, poetry, and songs;
- inspiration from the life of the preacher, the congregation, and pastoral care situations;
- holidays, sports, and what people are thinking about;
- cycles of seasons and what is going on in nature;
- the digital/technological context of life today.

From my experience of both preaching and listening to sermons, I recommend a natural flow between A and B content. Usually it seems that the listener can handle only a paragraph or two of religious B content without a return to an example or reference from everyday life. This, of course, can't be a prescription since each sermon has its own flow, organization, and purpose. David Lose, a well-known writer on preaching, has a similar way to think about the content of preaching. He suggests that preachers are addressing secular people today. In other words, since the Enlightenment, our concerns are of this world and whether our lives make sense and have meaning, purpose, and coherency. Most of us do not share Martin Luther's worry whether we will find a merciful and forgiving God in the afterlife. Rather, we seek a life in this world that has worth and value. Lose believes that most people realize existentially that what was once satisfying to us now leaves us empty, and that there must be something more to life, "a purposeful and meaningful goal toward which we strive."[17]

Lose is concerned about recent research showing that many church-goers do not have a sense of Christian vocation in their lives. "That is, they struggle to believe that what they do matters to God, or the church. Up to this point, in other words, their faith has provided little help in discovering hope, meaning, and purpose in their lives."[18] Lose believes that the Sunday sermon is the unique place where preachers can help people awaken to God's presence not only in creation, but in the diverse relationships and roles in which they find themselves.

How do preachers accomplish this? Lose notes that most preaching he observes is in one or two zones of people's life in the world. Preachers often focus on the *congregational zone*, making connections with what is going on in an individual congregation's ministry, budget, outreach, and programming. The other is what he calls "the global zone," in which the preacher addresses issues like hunger, natural disasters, or justice concerns such as racism, immigration, and ecology. Lose clearly emphasizes that both of these zones are essential theologically, ethically, and pastorally. Yet he also makes the point that what is missing is everything between—the zone in which we live most of our lives. "Jobs, looking for a job, relationships, parenting, managing too many things at once, money, family, school, hobbies, volunteering, the media, local current events—that is, the stuff that constitutes our daily lives—often seems to be painfully absent from

17. Lose, *Preaching at the Crossroads*, 66.
18. Ibid., 66.

most of our preaching." Lose emphasizes he is not calling for therapeutic sermons, but sermons that "help us see how these ancient stories offer us a lens, a perspective that helps us make sense of some of the ordinary and mundane things that make up most of our lives."[19]

Becoming Fully Human

Lose talks about the zone where people live their lives. That is what I have called "A content." Whatever term we use, how can preachers better make these important connections? It is sometimes said that rabbis and pastors are theologians in residence within a congregation. Their calling is to interpret ancient texts and to help people find God in their lives. Yet, pastors are also reflectors in residence and have a wonderful and unique opportunity to make spiritual connections for people in a time when personal reflection is on the wane. That means that the preacher must be self-aware and intentionally seek to live an authentic life, deeply aware of both the grace and struggle of daily existence.

I have often half-joked that if a preacher's sermons are to include references to movies, television, and the things our people are watching or thinking about, they could consider it part of their work to attend a film on a work weekday. I must say that I haven't done this very often, but I strongly believe that reading, keeping up with the news, and growing in self-awareness and societal analysis are as important as our study of the Scriptures. With real-world experience and reflection, the preacher will be able to translate the law-gospel dialectic in terms that will resonate with our hearers. From my seminary days, I still remember a preaching book by Herman Stuempfle in which he defined one aspect of preaching the law as being aware of the "mirror of existence."[20] Only when we can articulate the issues and needs of people today can we announce the gospel of Christ in ways that are creative, fresh, and relevant for these times. In other words, the preacher's reflective spirit invites hearers into some unplugged moments to consider how the themes presented intersect with their lives.

Even if you are not a religious leader, you can encourage your pastor and other spiritual leaders to nurture and maintain times of reflection and renewal in their busy lives so they access a deep reservoir on which to draw for preaching. Amid a constant barrage of alerts leading to wired

19. Ibid., 76.
20. Stuempfle, *Preaching Law and Gospel*, 23.

connectivity, it is my hope that communities of faith can point people to a deeper wisdom flowing from connections that are not draining of energy, but bear the fruits of love, peace, and a deeper reverence for the earth and its many peoples.

By now I hope it is clear that I am advocating that congregations—in their worship and preaching, in particular—be places that assist people in reflecting on their lives, and that equip them not only to connect to God, but to become more fully human through connecting with others. I urge religious leaders to take seriously their call to be reflectors in residence, pointing people to values such as authenticity, gratitude, and generosity. I can't resist quoting the well-known phrase by Irenaeus: "the glory of God is the human person fully alive." In a world marked by ubiquitous digital connectivity, guarding our essential humanity is certainly worth our time and effort, both as individuals and faith communities. And since most of us start with the self, the next chapter is appropriately called "Selfie."

SPIRITUAL PRACTICES

1. If you are a preacher, how do you nurture times for personal reflection in your life? For some, journaling, spiritual direction, or sacred conversation with a trusted friend or colleague provide such opportunities. When you listen to sermons, consider whether they lead you to deeper reflection on your faith and overall life context. Provide some feedback to your pastor or colleague, perhaps with both affirmations and suggestions.

2. Does the liturgy in your church allow space for reflection or is it wall-to-wall sound? Consider brief moments of silence or other ways for people to enjoy some unplugged moments to reflect on themes from the Scriptures, sermon, or liturgical occasion.

8

Selfie

Striving Toward Community

DO YOU REMEMBER THE first time you were able to take a selfie with your phone? Though selfies are essentially self-referential—we see and arrange ourselves in a photograph that we take ourselves—they are most often shared with family and friends on social media. Though the selfie may represent the individualism of our times, many of the pictures are viewed within a larger community. What is the relationship of self to community in an age of Facebook and Instagram? And what does any of this have to do with belonging to a church community and engaging in worship? Does communal ritual provide something that we can't find online or in our in-dividual spiritual searching? After a personal story about self-awareness, I will consider the challenge of finding and building community within a culture and pattern of social media that emphasize individualism. Those searching for a community of faith often call it "church shopping." Though it is difficult to generalize what undergirds the search, I will explore the benefits of not just perusing but belonging to a congregation. Before we go there, here is a personal reflection to lead us from selfie to self.

Starting with the Self

I was interviewing at a church. They asked me to describe myself. I would not have "come out" as an introvert if I felt strongly that the position—or, as we in ministry are more prone to say, the call—was a right match for me. From the beginning of the interview process I had been ambivalent but wanted to remain open to what might unfold. I thrive in midsize congregations in which I know everyone by name and can form meaningful relationships with nearly all of the parishioners. I had been on the staff of a two-thousand-member congregation. I appreciated the resources available, and even the number of people that would almost certainly show up for a new class, worship service, or any event. At the same time, it had been difficult for me to pass folks on Sunday mornings and not know their name. Instead of "Hey, John," it sometimes had to be, "Good morning."

Back to that call process. Since I wasn't sure whether I felt a sense of call to that place, I had nothing to lose in being completely open: so I decided to come out as an introvert. In an outgoing and transparent way, I defined the term introvert, at least as it is used in the well-known Myers-Briggs Type Indicator. I made sure they knew that I am a very social person, and that relationships are deeply significant to me. I am energized by small groups and one-on-one conversations, while also valuing time alone to recharge my batteries. I appreciate solitude and time for reading and reflection. I am very outgoing in preaching, presiding, and teaching, and in conversations, I told the call committee. In other words, *introvert* may be the term by which I define myself (like a selfie snapshot), yet others in the community may experience me differently in my public role and experience a great deal of extroverted energy in my personality. After all, we all take on different roles in different contexts and communities.

I am not sure that some committee members heard my explanation. As soon I used the word *introvert*, I could see the face of at least one committee member drop. What did he just say? He is a pastor and an introvert? How would that fly in our congregation? Of course, there are plenty of introverted pastors and comedians and movie stars, for that matter. In fact, in a recent seminary class that I taught, there were more introverts than extroverts. It's just that, without spinning out a definition, I would guess that a number of church folk assume that an introvert would be awkward around people, lack a strong sense of self and the outgoing social skills needed to lead a congregation. My life experience has led to growth in self-awareness, or what is sometimes called "inner work." Self-awareness is different than selfishness. In fact, some would say that before we can form authentic relationships with others, we need to be centered and secure in ourselves. The Myers-Briggs Type Indicator is one tool among others that helps people grow in self-understanding so they can thrive in their relationships with a variety of personality types in work, marriage, and other communal settings. I find this tool particularly helpful in understanding extroversion and introversion.

As an introvert I am usually a private person. I remember the first time I heard that people created profiles on dating websites or had Facebook pages all about themselves. I was somewhat intimidated by the concept of a dating profile, but when I found myself single in my mid-forties that did not stop me from attempting to capture my essence in an online page all about me. It was both exciting and terrifying. Facebook, Twitter, and other sites now take self-revelation to a whole new level as people broadcast their lives—events, pictures, feelings, news—through posts. It's no surprise that there would eventually be a way for us to take and post our own picture on social media sites—the selfie.

Self and Community

As much as we are motivated by our own needs and concerns, however, we are still social animals. Based on their unique interests or life circumstances, some people spend hours each day on social media. This networking enables them to feel more connected to others and various kinds of communities.

We often hear about the individualism of our times. It's not that we weren't concerned about ourselves before. In fact, it is often mentioned that Eastern cultures place more value on society and social connections while we in the West prize the individual. Baby Boomers began hearing themselves referred to as the "Me" generation back in the 1970s. Technology has only accelerated the tendency toward self-centeredness that had already been present in our social context for decades and has extended it to subsequent generational groups. In fact, millennials are sometimes referred to as "Generation Me."

I wonder how individualism—and our selfie age—affects involvement in organized religion. There is no need to rehearse the dire situation of the institutional church these days. There is great concern for the future of congregations, seminaries, denominations, publishing houses, and other faith-based organizations. Clearly, the financial viability of these institutions is at the heart of much worry and strategizing. Money is not the only worry, though. If seeking connection through community, in some way or another, is still important to people today, why are fewer people seeking it in church? There is no simple answer to that question. For now, I will simply observe that our relationship to technology, along with other social changes, is creating weaker ties to institutions of all types. A member of my congregation who serves as an usher for the Chicago Symphony Orchestra reminds me it's not just churches; a lot of organizations are facing challenging futures. Many who attend the orchestra's performances are seniors, and it is hard to attract a younger audience. Because technology allow us to listen to music anytime or anyplace through online services like Pandora and Spotify, is there less desire to attend a live concert? Though this may be true to some extent, there still are concerts and other public events that draw thousands of excited and enthusiastic people to them.

Think about the various communities of which you are part. An East African proverb says, "I am because we are, and because we are, therefore I am." Or recall the title of Hillary Clinton's book from the 1990s, *It Takes a Village*, noting all the various communities important in rearing a child in our society. We speak of the "African American community," the "gun rights community," or the "early music community." All of us need a community of which we are a part. Despite the rugged individualism in our country's DNA, it's hard to argue against any of the benefits of community:

> People are both healthier and happier when they are part of a well-functioning community. Not only does genuine community provide value, roots, connectedness, and stability, for each individual, but community is also good for society. Communities provide a glue that holds society together, and those communities oriented toward a "common good" can create an ethos that extends out in ripple fashion.[1]

Our ties to institutions are much looser than several decades ago. However, in today's highly partisan atmosphere, we most often associate with people who share our overall worldview. We cannot simply blame politicians for this situation. There are new social realities behind such partisan self-identification.

Our notion of community is changing. Much of it has to do with how we get our news and relate to social media. Columnist and writer David Brooks posits that in healthy societies people are "members of a family, a neighborhood, school, civic organization, hobby group, company, faith, regional culture, nation, continent, and world. Each layer of life is nestled in the others to form a varied but coherent whole."[2] Following World War

1. Mercadante, *Beliefs without Borders*, 156.
2. Brooks, "How to Fix Politics."

II there was a gradual movement away from membership in a number of communities to an emphasis on individual autonomy. While we now tend to relate closely a small circle of family and friends—and tangentially to hundreds of Facebook "friends"—we are rarely connected to the diversity of middle-ring relationships that neighborhoods and churches once provided. Brooks argues that by having fewer ways of self-identification, "people put politics at the center of their psychological, emotional and even spiritual life." The result is that politics becomes too important because we don't have the ability to compromise or to view life other than from our particular perspective or worldview.[3] Brooks makes a compelling case, indirectly, for the importance of belonging to a community of faith, a contrast to the pattern and tide of recent decades.

More Nones

Young adults are not attending church these days. At least, that is what multiple studies are showing. That is not what I see at my church. My congregation is in a very transient, fluid neighborhood, so most of the time there are newcomers, including a steady flow of young adults dropping in for worship. Perhaps they are looking for a church or simply testing the waters; it's hard to tell. Maybe they're not even sure what they are looking for. Many of the newcomers are hesitant or at least slow to make themselves known, to sign the worship registration slip, or to become a member of the congregation. Yet, contrary to the idea that young people are not attending church, they do attend, either regularly or from time to time.

This lack of clear commitment, for some, isn't a surprise in light of the growing number of religiously unaffiliated people (sometimes called "nones") that we have heard a lot about the past five years. Some describe the nones as the fastest growing religious group, so to speak, in the country. A report by the Pew Forum on Religion and Public Life offers four possible explanations for the rise of the unaffiliated over the past several decades.[4] The first is the perception by young adults, in particular, that religion is too closely aligned with conservative politics. Many millennials came of age around 1990 when Christianity was often linked with the Religious Right, particularly in the press. With gay rights and abortion as lightening rod issues, many young adults simply found organized religion to be "judgmen-

3. Ibid.
4. Pew Forum, *"Nones" on the Rise.*

tal, homophobic, hypocritical, and too political."[5] A second theory names the delay in marriage and parenthood for young adults' lack of affiliation today.[6] The third theory, represented by Robert Putman in his well-known phrase "bowling alone," suggests that as Americans grow more individualistic and isolated, they are less likely to be involved in civic and communal activities like church.[7]

Lastly, some people link an increase of nones in the United States to a rise in secularization and economic development around the globe. Though predictions made several decades ago that religion would be nearly non-existent by the twenty-first century have not materialized, "gradual secularization is to be expected in a generally healthy, wealthy, orderly society." Though some Pew reports reveal that in many places in the world there is a correlation between a country's economic health and religious participation (greater wealth correlates with less religion), the United States until recently was the primary exception to that rule since American church attendance has been consistently strong. The current increase in the unaffiliated in the United States leads some theorists to conclude that America is becoming gradually more secular and closer to the situation in Europe.[8]

Church Shopping

Despite nones being on the rise, there clearly are plenty of people searching for something in our religions communities. It may not be on our terms, such as membership and financial commitment, as noted earlier—or on our timetable—yet I continue to marvel at the number of new people coming through our doors. Many of them, I realize, are "church shopping." As much as I don't like the term, it is probably what I would say if I were looking for a church. And it certainly is the term used when I hear people talk of their experience of searching for a church home. Many of these church shoppers will visit a number of parishes, sometimes of different denominations, until they find one that meets their needs or tastes, occasionally scoring congregations in areas such as music, preaching, building, and friendliness. You can now find church reviews on Yelp. My congregation, among others, has been reviewed by *Mystery Worshipper*—an anonymous

5. Putnam and Campbell, *American Grace*, 120–21.

6. Wuthnow, *After the Baby Boomers*, 51–70.

7. Putnam, *Bowling Alone*.

8. Pew Forum, *"Nones" on the Rise*, 31.

blog by someone who drops in unannounced and writes about a church's building, hospitality, liturgy, music, and preaching.[9]

In today's consumer culture, many churches consider marketing techniques as a way to invite people to join them for worship. So let's consider the role that advertising has in shaping our identities as individuals. Our tastes and shopping patterns are now tracked online so that marketers can tailor their advertisements for each individual. Who hasn't browsed a website only to find a sidebar ad for the product appearing the next day on our computer? The point of the ads is usually not to detail the specifics of the product but to promise that the use of a product will make you feel better about yourself, alleviate pain, broaden sex appeal, delay aging, or deepen self-esteem and happiness. Having wishes and desires fulfilled is merely a few clicks away when one is online. At the same time, advertisers create dissatisfaction in consumers so that we will always desire a new and improved product. The "creation of dissatisfaction has to go beyond the notion that who one *is* is inadequate . . . the message is simple: You are inadequate, so buy more things."[10] In other words, the emptiness we feel gets connected with a perceived inadequacy. We turn to products—and any number of things—believing that they will offer us lasting satisfaction.

More and more we experience this phenomenon in our relationship with gadgets and devices. Devoted Apple fans await the release of a new iPhone with great anticipation, despite the fact that most of us already own a fully functioning smartphone. Advertising leads us to believe that we *need* the most recent product, that it will make us cool, make our work more efficient, and ultimately bring more happiness. There is no question that, for many, these products indeed do bring delight and bring a kind of joy, yet it is only a matter of time until the newer, faster, sleeker version is desired.

In our society religion has also become commodified. The marketing of church correlates with the preference that many people have for a spirituality that can be customized to suit their own needs. When institutions are suspect, people become seekers in a spiritual marketplace, drawing things, ideas, or practices from diverse traditions while rejecting components not found meaningful or relevant. It's the concept of bricolage that we explored in an earlier chapter. One size does not fit all these days. Think of it like creating our own playlist of music we like, while discarding the songs from an album (for those of us who remember the concept of an album) that

9. "Holy Trinity, Chicago," *Mystery Worshipper*, January 10, 2016.

10. Brunk, "Consumer Culture and the Body," 292.

we don't find appealing.[11] In most ways, this may seem inappropriate and inauthentic for religion.

At the same time, if the goal is to help people find genuine community, one could ask whether the contemporary church needs to be aware of the positive aspects of marketing and advertising as well. If a particular community exhibits integrity it will work against the natural distrust of institutions held by many these days. Advertising then becomes a way for churches to invite others to a more meaningful life. David Lose believes that congregations could learn some important lessons from Apple stores. Lose takes "Ten Things You Can Learn from the Apple Store," originally written for those in business and industry, and makes applications for worship and congregational life. Surprisingly, most of his points are helpful and do not merely smack of consumerism. For example, Lose believes the hands-on experience in Apple stores can lead congregations to value multisensory liturgy, and that in the same way as an uncluttered, brightly lit, open store appeals to the buying brain, congregations should look to simplify their space and calendars.[12]

It is important to note, too, that as technology is morally neutral, the same is true of shopping. After all, humans are essentially consumers. We need food, clothing, money, and other resources. Consumerism is an endless drive to acquire more than we need. When our purchases and our products deepen the sense of relationships, of community, and of what it means to be human, they should be celebrated. One of my parishioners notes how her iPhone helps her to be closer to her adult children through texts and photos. Facebook has deepened ties to high school friends, colleagues, and both old and new communities. My congregation has used many marketing strategies in designing our website, e-newsletter, and a promotional video. We have learned how important it is to understand how people use the Internet, Facebook, and email today, for example, rather than simply assuming that what we created a decade ago continues to be appropriate. Certainly religion, church, or God are not a *product* that we want people to buy in a literal sense. We need to ask, however, what we hope to be the result of people's experience of church. I would hope that it is a life that is more connected spiritually, not only to God, but to all that it means to be human.

---

11. Miller, "Liturgy and Popular Culture," 163–64.

12. Lose, "10 Things the Church Can Learn," para. 6–15.

Spiritual Marketplace

What are people shopping for when they visit churches and what are churches marketing? If consumerism has almost religious overtones in the United States, sprawling malls, sports stadiums, and banking towers might be considered our temples today. In a context in which individual choice is paramount, *marketplace* is an apt way to describe the plethora of religious and spiritual options available to seekers today. While consumerism seeks to fulfill an individual's desire, "faith offers satisfaction through desire for the Other."[13]

Today's spiritual marketplace has evolved over the past half century. Beginning in the 1950s, America moved from a nation with strong loyalty to religious institutions, usually involving a lifetime in one tradition, to a context in which individual preference is paramount. For example, writer Diana Butler Bass tells of a coffee executive who reveals that at his establishment there are eighty-two thousand possible drink options and combinations available from his menu.[14] Bass sees making choices from a host of possibilities as the state of our religious marketplace: "When faced with such a wide array of ways to connect with God, to love's one neighbor, and to practice faith, we all now have to decide for ourselves. Choice in religion is just what it is. There is no escaping it."[15] I find myself overwhelmed with the quantity of options for books and music that I can instantaneously download, and believe that I am more content when offered fewer choices.

Religious institutions need to offer something of value to those who attend and contribute financially. Otherwise, the people will go elsewhere, or in a growing number of cases, nowhere at all. This reality is close to home for many pastors today. On the second Sunday in my current congregation, eighteen years ago, there were about forty people in the worship service. The next day I overheard my administrator comment that "it is hard to keep a church open with offerings like we had that day." Though money should not guide the church's ministry, there was a sense that the challenge of sustainability forced our congregation to consider what type of church would be relevant in our context. For us that meant we needed to be aware of the unique concerns, needs, and gifts that urban professionals brought with them to church. Even now I ask some of these people to talk

13. Spinks, *Worship Mall*, Kindle loc. 308–14.

14. Bass, *Christianity After Religion*, 41.

15. Ibid., 46–47.

about their perceptions of organized religion, I get an earful of all the baggage and the negative experiences that they and others carry with them. This information has been significant as I considered the kind of outreach needed in our context.

The concept of marketing church also reveals that though a number of congregations in an area have the same denominational label, there may be significant differences in pastoral style, music, worship, and mission, and demographics. Each congregation does not need to do everything well. What may be more important is for a community of faith to find its unique niche in their particular context and then use online outreach strategies to let people know what that niche is. On one hand, church shopping can represent the downside of individualism. If I don't find a community to suit my needs, I will not attend at all. On the other hand, I cannot deny that my congregation is trying to offer something appealing, with authenticity and integrity that may speak to deeper, even unknown desires in people.

Sociologists note that our country has always had a "dynamic religious landscape" and there has always been a "constant stream of innovation with U.S. religion."[16] Are there creative ways to woo the nones back to mainline denominations? Since many young adults still believe in God, some suggest that the many unaffiliated young adults could represent an inviting target for religious entrepreneurs.[17] Some of these disaffected folks might be won over by churches that emphasize inclusiveness and a progressive theological stance[18]—certainly something I have seen in my congregation. Many of our new members respond most to a spirit of openness and acceptance that seems to be a great contrast with their earlier church experiences. Another example would be Urban Village Church in Chicago, a United Methodist ministry to young adults, which once used this tag line: "We love doubters. We love believers. Come see how we do church differently." Some authors are hopeful that "the consistent pattern of religious entrepreneurship in America" will lead to more innovations, "mostly incremental, mostly within local congregations, but always inventive."[19]

Another diagnosis, however, is more somber. If people's spiritual search today is simply a desire for self-fulfillment without an awareness of the needs of others, then the act of choosing goods that merely reflect one's

---

16. Putnam and Campbell, *American Grace*, 162.
17. Ibid., 176.
18. Ibid., 176–77.
19. Ibid., 179.

lifestyle confirms the identity of the self primarily as consumer. "Shorn of its disruptive challenge, religion becomes a mere coping mechanism to smooth the contradictions of a middle-class status quo . . . It supplies the veneer of meaning and conviction we desire, without disrupting the underlying form of our lives."[20] Selfies and self-expression are the signs of the times. Yet our spiritual traditions speak of offering oneself for others. We model our lives on the sacrificial love of Jesus for the sake of a world in need. We may be marketing church, but we are inviting people to a countercultural way of life. In the midst of community, our self-centered lives are disrupted as we gather around a gospel message that speaks of the lowly and poor lifted up, and the hungry filled with good things. The words of the Magnificat—the song of Mary—move us from selfies to a community of faith that serves the world.

Communal Body

In the liturgy of baptism a self is placed within a community. We could even say that a self finds identity and purpose within the community. A countercultural message, indeed: it is not only about me. The assembly itself—a community—therefore "constitutes the most basic symbol of Christian worship."[21] Not only are the texts of the New Testament addressed to the plural "you," and meant to be read in assemblies, the basic elements of the liturgy—creeds, calendars, texts, and hymns, for example—are meant for communal expression.[22] Yet, liturgical theologian Gordon Lathrop describes how, in the midst of today's spiritual marketplace, religion is seen as the "private concern of an individual . . . A book of prayers held in my hand or an electronic forum about private rituals consulted on my own time can reinforce in me the sense that my religion is largely my own individual affair."[23]

Though individuals will have their unique experiences of the liturgy, worship is by its very nature communal. "Just as personal experiences of God happen in our individual bodies, we meet the divine communally in our collective body. It is *together* that we constitute the body of Christ, and God is mediated to us through our encounter with one another."[24] We are

20. Miller, "Liturgy and Popular Culture," 291.
21. Lathrop, *Holy People*, 21.
22. Ibid., 21.
23. Ibid., 24.
24. Long, *Worshiping Body*, 18.

baptized into a "social body," yet an embodied, physical one as well. "We make present a *body*, a *people*, an *assembly* that itself claims to be the body of Christ, flesh of his flesh and bone of his bone. In ritual—in liturgy and worship—the Church *becomes* the very thing it creates: the body of Christ, member for member."[25] Through the various bodily rituals in the baptismal rite, communal identity gets written on our very bodies: "as the community that put on Christ in baptism, or perhaps that has had Christ 'written' on us so physically through water, oil, and garments, we gather as the ongoing 'enfleshment,' the 'in-habitants' of the Body of Christ in the world."[26]

This communal identity does not negate the unique gifts and perspectives that each person brings to a community of faith, yet what is less easily recognized is the inherent power that ritual experience has in shaping communal identity and mission. Though technology makes us more connected to and aware of the greater world, it can also seem that we are more isolated and individualistic than ever—a group of selfies. As meeting together in community becomes increasingly countercultural, I wonder if there is an even greater benefit from such gathering.

Ritual Forms Community

By its very nature, ritual has power to bring people together and create and unite a community with deep, even emotional bonds. Consider the raw energy at a sporting event, parade, or political convention. My congregation is a few blocks from Wrigley Field, the historic stadium of the Chicago Cubs, and I am always intrigued with the sense of ritual I observe when I attend a baseball game. "Ritual controls emotion while releasing it, and guides it while letting it run."[27] Whether the joy of a wedding celebration or the anguished grief of a funeral, ritual provides a way to move through these life passages and the often mixed emotions that are stirred. The presence of music, movement, gestures, and communal solemnity afford needed emotional contours that few other experiences in life can provide.

Cultural anthropologists use the term *communitas* to describe the very essence of ritual. In contrast to the term *community*, which usually denotes a village, town, or neighborhood, *communitas* is "an essential and

25. Mitchell, "Amen Corner," 71–72.
26. Anderson, "Liturgy: Writing Faith in the Body," 175.
27. Driver, *Magic of Ritual*, 152–56.

generic human bond, without which there could be no society."[28] *Communitas* creates a ritual state in which participants experience a kind of unity with and among themselves, in which "the boundary between individuals and their surroundings, especially others participating in ritual with them, may seem to dissolve."[29]

It is ironic that there are few ritual occasions in our contemporary context that both unite and transform a group of participants. I question whether virtual experiences can ever provide such life-changing experiences of *communitas*. If people are not connected to organized religion, they may not be seeking ritual engagement at all. Tom Driver, a scholar of ritual, suggests that people in privileged Western societies rarely experience the *communitas* of ritual because they may be fearful of losing what they have. He wonders whether we want to be reminded of our bond with humanity because it would cause us to identify with those most vulnerable in society. When we ritualize the "dream for a common humanity," it can threaten our very way of life.[30]

Worshipping in community makes a difference. Participating in the same bodily rituals with others provides a countercultural understanding of self. When an assembly faces the deep truths of the human condition and our common vulnerability before God and the world, there is a transformation, a change of orientation: "a change from being the one in control, the one in charge, to being the worshiper; a change from being the user and exploiter to being the reverencer and lover; a change from being the one who has all the answers to being the one who is comfortable with mystery and questions; a change from being the master to being the seeker."[31]

Let's return to the selfie one last time. In the past our photograph was nearly always taken by someone else. We needed someone else to help us create the memory of a special occasion. It was a ritual. "Stand over there. Mary, move closer to your sister. Say cheese." Now we do it ourselves, like so much in our digital lives. Selfies are self-referential. We don't need anyone. And in this change we lose something in special occasions marked by the relationship of poser and photographer. Looking at a selfie is not the same experience as looking at an old photograph your mother took of you unwrapping a Christmas present. In worship such rituals are restored. The

---

28. Turner, *Ritual Process*, 83.
29. Rappaport, *Ritual and Religion*, 220.
30. Driver, *Magic of Ritual*, 165.
31. Huck, ed., *Toward Ritual Transformation*, 19–20.

church year includes fasts and festivals. These are communal events that deepen ties to one another and to the essence of our faith. And because many of these rituals have been the same for centuries, they tie us to a community of the past, extending ourselves beyond the present moment. For those of us who have attended church all our lives, the rituals connect us to our past selves—such as receiving ashes on Ash Wednesday. This connection can take us from self-absorption to moments of grace and openness.

In a world of advertising designed to meet needs we did not even know we had, and in a context of selfies and endless self-expression, the church invites people to something different. We experience the power of ritual in the midst of a community with all its diversity and dysfunction, its potential and frustrations. Certainly, we need community in a variety of contexts. What is less acknowledged by many today is our need for ritual and the transformation it provides. We are stronger together. What community means for finding one's purpose in life is the theme of the next chapter.

SPIRITUAL PRACTICES

1. Though many spiritual practices are done alone, reflect on specific practices that you do as a group. What are the benefits of singing in a choir, serving on a team, or volunteering together at soup kitchen, for example?

2. Consider ways that communal ritual can be incorporated into the life of your congregation, family, classroom, or another community.

3. When you are looking for a new congregation, how could what is called "church shopping" be viewed as a spiritual practice? How would that shift of perspective affect your language or your goals for the process?

9

GPS

Mapping Purpose

THE JOURNEY IS A great metaphor for life. Oh, if we only had a spiritual GPS to guide us. A pulsing dot would reveal where we presently are in our lives. Once a route is determined, we would receive specific directions: where we are going and how to get there, who we are becoming, and what we are doing with this one life we have been given.

Even when we affirm that we are embodied and mortal, connected to God and various communities—as we have explored in earlier chapters—we still must discern what gets us up in the morning. Whether we are a student or a retired person, working in a chosen field or simply earning money to make a living, we continue to wrestle with questions of purpose. Throughout the various stages of our lives, most of us want to be engaged in activities or work that is meaningful and makes a difference in our lives or the lives of others.

This chapter will explore how worship and spirituality assist us in discovering and living out our purpose—sometimes defined as our mission or vocation—in life. Sent from the liturgy, we live out our baptismal vocation in the various life contexts in which we find ourselves.

I can think of several times in life when I wondered what direction I was going and what choices I really had in the process. Such times of searching are called "discernment" in spirituality. When I was in my mid-thirties and underemployed, I wondered whether I would ever find the right match for my professional gifts and passions. When I found myself single in my forties, I worried whether I would ever find the significant other for whom I longed. There are so many things about my situation that I could have never imagined twenty years ago—both unbearable loss and indescribable joy. I have been rejected in ways that shook me to the core and delighted by circumstances that surprised me and brought great joy to my life. When I was in the midst of those experiences, I wish I had had GPS to provide directions. Unfortunately, that's not how the journey of life works.

A significant experience of discernment for me was determining how long was appropriate to stay in my current call. Often a long-term pastorate is defined as staying in one congregation longer than ten years. I am well over that. My GPS dot has been at the same location much longer than I have had any gadgets equipped with GPS! During my tenth through fifteenth years, I wondered whether it would be best for the congregation and my own spiritual growth to interview for other calls, and open myself up to new challenges and adventures. Yet I continued to return to the good fit in my current call. Since it is a very transient congregation, there are barely twenty people whose presence preceded my arrival. Though I have stayed put, dozens and dozens of people have moved on to other communities, other cities, and other jobs. Perhaps that is why the Farewell and Godspeed liturgy is so emotional for me. We continue to say goodbye to young adults who were part of our congregation in a very formative time, and we send them forth on new journeys related to their career, family, or children.

One colleague told me that he solved his restlessness and need for new challenges by moving to a new job every seven or so years. The Benedictine value of stability is about staying put and remaining committed to a certain community, a certain place, a certain vocation. Rather than seeking a new job to provide variety and spice things up a bit, I sought ways to reinvent myself in creative ways. For several years, I led the spiritual formation program at the Lutheran seminary in Chicago. Next I pursued and completed a Doctor of Ministry degree. Finally, I invited my congregation to consider a mission initiative by offering a Saturday night service in the South Loop as there were no ELCA churches in downtown Chicago.

I have to admit that the discernment period that preceded each of those creative periods was difficult. I wanted to be open to God's leading through the process. I knew I needed to trust the deep wisdom within me. It took a lot of energy to gently hold the various opportunities that presented themselves to me. Were they a good fit? Should I interview for the position? Could my spouse and I uproot ourselves and move to a new state? Again, there was no GPS for such life questions. I had to go through the process to discern what each next step would be.

Speaking of GPS, are you old enough to remember paper maps? Now we rely on GPS to get us where we need to go. For example, the City Planner app will give me a number of public transportation options for getting around Chicago—or other cities to which I travel—and will let me know when the next bus or train is due to arrive anywhere in the city. When driving, Waze suggests the best route to take based on current traffic. As much as I love these new apps, I fear that in allowing a voice in my phone to get me from place to place I have no idea how I get somewhere, and would be unable to travel anywhere without a GPS function.

Simon Garfield, author of a book about maps, himself uses map apps, but grieves that we are losing the beauty and romance of paper maps, and the tactile joy of folding one up. I found his comments about losing a "sense of how big the world is" haunting. In an NPR interview he argued that maps on electronic devices give us the feeling that "'It's all about me' . . . It's a terribly egocentric way of looking at the world. So I think the view of where we are in the world, in the history of the world, is changing. And I think in a way it's one of the biggest, if not *the* biggest impacts of the digital and technological revolution."[1] When I look at a map app, the little pulsing dot always identifies where I am as center of the world. It is hard to gain perspective of the greater whole.

We want to know where we are going and how we will get there—as we literally or metaphorically traverse the roads of life. Part of our spiritual journey is discovering our purpose in life. To what or to whom do we give our lives? How do we invest our time and financial resources? What brings joy and satisfaction? A retired person in his late seventies told me he was still trying to figure out what he was going to do with his life.

Since a GPS map places us at the center of everything, it may seem counterintuitive to turn to a community, a tradition, or even to God to assist us in the task of discovering our purpose and call. When religion is no longer trusted as a dependable source of authority, that life situation creates even more challenges. What is the purpose of the church in these changing times?

Navigating the Purpose of the Church

If we look at today's religious landscape, it is no surprise that many people name themselves Christian, but have no room for the church in their lives,

1. Garfield, "Mapping a History of the World," para. 6–7.

at least in any significant or regular way. A spiritual inward journey, yes. Organized religion, not so much. Another way to describe this current context is *post-Christian* or *post-Christendom*, defined as "the culture which emerges as the Christian faith loses coherence within a society that has been definitively shaped by the Christian story and as the institutions that have been developed to express Christian convictions decline in influence."[2]

One problem, of course, is that we often evaluate a congregation's success at fulfilling its purpose—or mission—by the number of people in worship or the amount of money in the offering plate (or given online as is more and more the case these days). As one consultant said, we count "bucks and butts." Then how do we measure its ministry after a congregation departs from worship and members live their faith during the week? In other words, do we evaluate ministry with the GPS dot centered on the church building or on where people are living their everyday lives? Church consultant Del Rendle agrees that we need to continue counting in our churches, but ultimately ministry isn't about membership or organizational growth, it is about the transformation of a person or community. In other words, changed lives that come from "an encounter with the presence and story of Christ."[3] Rendle believes that churches, like other nonprofits, do not articulate the difference they are trying to make in people's lives and get hung up on the wrong things.[4] In attempting to be churchy and even theological, we may not always be making a connection with people where they work and live, and with the real questions and struggles that define their lives.

Being Sent

To the question of purpose, "Where am I going with my life?" the church answers, "You are sent." Though sometimes lost in the way we speak of mission statements today, the etymology of the word *mission* shows that it means *to be sent*. When I was growing up, I had a vague idea of a missionary as someone who brought the truth of the gospel to those in faraway countries who hadn't heard the good news of Jesus. In recent decades a different and clearer ecumenical consensus regarding mission has developed. At the heart of mission theology today is the notion of *missio Dei*, the mission of God. God's very nature is missional and is rooted in the Holy

2. Kreider and Kreider, *Worship and Mission*, 15.

3. Rendle, *Doing the Math of Mission*, 11.

4. Ibid., 14.

Trinity: not only does the Father send the Son and the Spirit, "the church is sent by the Father and the Son to continue the mission of Jesus in the power of the Holy Spirit, that is, to be a witness of the kingdom of God until history is consummated in the full coming of the kingdom."[5] In other words, we follow in the way of Jesus who embodies God's mission, *missio Dei.*

There is a major paradigm shift from the idea that missionaries are sent to bring God to the unchristianized world to the belief that God is already at work in the world, whether we notice it or not. In this case, the GPS dot reveals where you are sent to serve: right where you are. What a contrast to seeing ourselves as the center of the world, or seeing ministry as primarily done only by clergy in church buildings. Rather, we are all called to serve the world wherever we are, wherever our dot is on any given day. All around us people are staring at their GPS devices, seeing the same dot we are, called to serve wherever they happen to be and to be mindful of God's presence in all things and in all places.

So it's not as if Christians are the only ones who can bring healing and restoration to places of ignorance and darkness. That proposition not only insults people of other religions and no religion, it also discounts the presence of divine action in creation and in the lives of all human beings. If God is missional, then God is at work not only in those designated "missionaries" and in religious people of good will, but in countless places and situations. "At their best, Christian missionaries have discovered that God is at work before they got there. And this is the task of Christians who participate in God's mission: to expect to find God at work and to be intently alert to what God is doing."[6]

God's purpose—mission—is one of healing, reconciling, liberating, and restoring the universe. Despite the brokenness in the world, some would say that the *missio Dei* is bringing God's *shalom* to every aspect of creation and human life. In other words, God's "project" is to bring all-encompassing wholeness in these three modes of life: humans with God, humans with creation, and humans with other humans.[7]

When a congregation gathers for worship in the context of its own GPS dot, it experiences the "formation and transformation of its culture," which then leads to bold mission in the world.[8] If the church participates in God's mission that is already happening in the world, the church loses

5. Lovas, "Mission-Shaped Liturgy," 353.

6. Kreider and Kreider, *Worship and Mission*, 49.

7. Ibid., 46.

8. Bliese and Gelder, *Evangelizing Church*, 74.

some of its power and control. Some would wonder if the church is even necessary when the locus of divine action is located in the world. Others question whether those in the church have done a good job of connecting worship and our calling to live in the world. The church has become comfortable with the familiar and has "allowed our faith to slip into hibernation. We have taken the gift for granted. And, in the meantime, there is a world that lies just outside our door, groaning in pain, hungry for anything that will fill it up and make it whole, wrecked by sin and longing to become everything it was created to be."[9]

So the mission GPS is leading to the world. That is the purpose—the holy calling—of the people of God. These days the term *public church* is sometimes used in this regard. Lutheran theologian Cynthia D. Moe-Lobeda writes of the challenges and opportunities of being a public church engaged in mission for the life of the world. She argues that most people are geared toward the private good, and what will ultimately benefit the individual rather than the public good. As an ethicist she believes that the morality of the privatized self demands more scrutiny today than the "moral condition of society." In an age of individualization, she concludes, "Amidst this turn to the private, the church of God is called to the *missio dei*, a public vocation for the sake of God's creation, the vast public."[10] It all depends upon whether we view the pulsing GPS dot as showing ourselves to be the center of the world or showing our current location in the world to be the center of our life's purpose.

So if our task is in the world, why go to church? Worship by its very nature teaches us to cast down idols, and perhaps the most dangerous one is a false sense of our own grandeur, or as Eugene Peterson puts it, "worship is the time and place that we assign for deliberate attentiveness to God—not because he's confined to time and place, but because our self-importance is so insidiously relentless that if we don't deliberately interrupt ourselves regularly we have no chances of attending to him at all at other times and in other places."[11] In other words, worshipping God changes us. Worship affects the way we interpret our GPS bubble and the way we view every aspect of life; "it transforms our political perspectives and the way we watch the news and spend our money."[12]

9. Ibid., 12.

10. Moe-Lobeda, *Public Church*, 12.

11. Peterson, *Leap Over a Wall*, 152–53.

12. Kreider and Kreider, *Worship and Mission*, 189.

Do We Need Worship for Mission?

Maybe everything I have said seems obvious to you. However, the challenge today is that many people do *not* see these potential benefits of "going to church," as they would call it. Is there a missing link in the way we talk about mission or about the purpose of being a part of a community of faith?

A remaining question is this: in a post-Christendom context, where will the people of God find the "insight and inspiration to participate in God's mission?"[13] Certainly some people can be energized by small groups, reading, political action, and volunteer activities; yet without intentionality and a break in our routine, might we lose perspective and become fixated on our own little GPS bubble? "Worship is the environment in which God's people . . . are sensitized to recognize the inbreaking of God's reign. Worship is the clarifying air that God's people breathe, enabling them to detect idolatry and to repudiate facile solutions."[14]

The Call of Your Life

A woman recently told me of her experience of filling out her parish's "Time and Talent" sheet during worship. The only items on the list were things like teaching Sunday school, singing in the choir, serving coffee hour, and volunteering at a food pantry. Yet this woman's life was already filled to the brim, and she came to church to find community, solace, and nourishment for her daily life. What she didn't hear being affirmed was the call to live in faith in the context of her everyday life and that what she was already doing was ministry. She needed acknowledgement of the mission of her GPS dot right where it was.

I tell my new members that my primary hope is not that they become good Lutherans or faithful church members, but that worship forms them to live their baptism in the context of their daily lives. In other words, the two most important things are worship and service in the world. All the congregational activities outside of worship are beneficial, but they are not the main thing. Of course, we need people to volunteer in our congregations, but I believe the primary role of the parish is to form the people of God for ministry in the various contexts in which they work, love, study, love, and pray.

13. Ibid., 58.
14. Ibid., 58.

Orthodox theologian Ion Bria talks about mission as the "liturgy after the liturgy," which is none other than the worshipper witnessing in "the common round of daily life."[15] Lutheran theology is rooted in the vocation of the baptized, or what is sometimes called the "priesthood of all believers." Lutheran author Foster McCurley gets specific about the ways the people of God live their faith in their everyday lives. "Nurses, physicians, housekeepers, dieticians, lawyers, scientists, bankers, construction workers, and social workers—the list is endless—all contribute to the well-being of God's creation. What is amazing about this work of God is that . . . human occupations serve God's purpose *whether they know it or not.*"[16]

In new member and confirmation classes and in liturgies in which the Affirmation of Baptism is celebrated, I often describe the following question, which is asked of those affirming the baptismal covenant, as a "job description" for the Christian. Note the references both to gathering in community for worship and service in the public sphere:

> Do you intend to continue in the covenant
> God makes with you in holy baptism:
> to live among God's faithful people,
> to hear the word of God and share in the Lord's supper,
> to proclaim the good news of God in Christ through word and deed,
> to serve all people, following the example of Jesus,
> and to strive for justice and peace in all the earth?[17]

In an era in which many people struggle with the belief systems of organized religion, this may be liberating news. Too often people have seen Christianity as subscribing to a system of beliefs and doctrines, rather than a way of life. Yet, as much as pastors talk about grand but simple things like baptismal vocation, ministry in everyday life, or even the classic Lutheran phrase "priesthood of all believers," it is rarely easy to know, let alone live fully, one's true calling or purpose in life. Sometimes we hear the pious prescription to simply follow Jesus and do as he did. On one hand, that is a good guideline, but on the other hand, we are not Jesus and our call is be fully ourselves. God has created us each with our unique DNA, passions, circumstances, and gifts. As spiritual writer Thomas Merton wisely wrote, everyone "has a vocation to be someone: but he must understand

15. Bria, *Liturgy After the Liturgy*, 87.
16. McCurley, *Go in Peace, Serve the Lord*, 21.
17. *Evangelical Lutheran Worship*, 237.

that in order to fulfill this vocation, he can only be one person: himself [or herself]."[18] Clearly there are critical times that we most seek wisdom or guidance in finding what we want or are able to do with our lives. These may include choosing a college major or vocational path, whether to accept a job, whom we should marry, whether to have children, and what to do in retirement. But I would wager that most of us are nearly always facing some kind of unease or at least questions about where we are going and the direction of our life. Perhaps the answers are more obvious than we think.

A book that has profoundly affected me and number of people I know has this provocative title: *The Great Work of Your Life: A Guide for the Journey to Your True Calling.* Using the Hindu spiritual classic called the *Bhagavad Gita*, Stephen Cope invites readers to consider their *dharma*, which can be defined as path, teaching, vocation, sacred duty, and ultimately the inner truth about themselves.[19] Cope proposes something that he believes will surprise most of us: most of the ordinary people he has studied initially believed that for them to live their dharma they would need to do something dramatic like quit selling shoes and move to Paris to study art. Actually, most people are very close to living their dharma already, but they don't name what is already in plain sight.[20] In other words, they don't look closely at their current GPS location and context. Plagued by things like doubt and procrastination, we fail to discover our dharma, the "peculiar and idiosyncratic" qualities as unique as our fingerprint that help us be true to "the subtle interior blueprint" of our soul.[21] Whether our dharma is revealed in something that brings a paycheck or in the great passion we pursue outside of so-called work, contexts will vary. Cope believes that continuing to pursue this truth about ourselves is the work of a lifetime, but a worthwhile effort, because "dharma gives us the one thing we need to be fully human: Each of us must have one domain, one small place on the globe where we can fully meet life—where we can meet it with every gift we have."[22] This sounds to me like the Christian understanding of the priesthood of all believers.

18. Merton, *No Man Is an Island*, 133.

19. Cope, *Great Work of Your Life*, xxi.

20. Ibid., xxvi.

21. Ibid., 21–22.

22. Ibid., 282.

Always to Places of Need

Whether we consider the church or the individual, our spiritual GPS always leads in one way or another to places of need. And usually wherever our dot is located, there will be people who are hurting in one way or another. When caught up in our personal pursuits it is easy to become blind to human suffering, yet it is precisely in places of suffering that grace may meet us most profoundly. We are sent to these places. In them we find our purpose. A prayer after Communion in *Evangelical Lutheran Worship* first mentions thanks for the feast set before us, and then asks that the Spirit "strengthen us to serve all in need and to give ourselves away as bread for the hungry."[23]

In a time when many churchgoers want a spirituality (and thus, sermons) that is therapeutic, it is a challenge for religious leaders to find ways to balance a message of grace and hope for those overwhelmed by the stress of life with one that calls a community to self-sacrifice for the sake of others. This tension needs to be held gently as ancient sacred texts are juxtaposed with contemporary realities. If God's mission is also for the privileged, then part of the divine surprise is that there is good news for those who know not material but spiritual poverty, even as they are called to raise their sights to the needs of a suffering humanity and needy world.

For those who practice the Christian faith and seek to follow in the way of Jesus, regular participation in the Sunday assembly is intrinsic for participating in God's purpose in the context of everyday life. Worship gathers and sends, forms and transforms, comforts and challenges the people of God as they encounter God's shalom break into their midst in Scripture, song, prayer, silence and Eucharist, and then join the work of liberation and healing in their respective communities. The GPS directions are simple: we go to church on Sundays and are then sent into our everyday lives from there. Part of being human is seeking purpose for our lives. Our faith shows us that the pulsing dot at the center of our electronic map does not mean that we are at the center of all things. Rather, the center reveals our purpose: we join God's work whenever and wherever we meet human needs. This leads us to the final chapter and how the divine presence in all of life gives us a sense of augmented reality.

23. *Evangelical Lutheran Worship*, 114.

SPIRITUAL PRACTICES

1. Reflect on the ways you live your baptismal faith. Using the formula in the *Evangelical Lutheran Worship* Affirmation of Baptism rite, consider ways you might grow in any of these areas: living among God's faithful people; hearing the word of God and sharing in the Lord's Supper; proclaiming the good news of God in Christ through word and deed; serving all people, following the example of Jesus; and striving for justice and peace in all the earth.

2. Consider how your congregation talks about stewardship, usually involving time, talent, and treasure. Does it honor the ways that you serve in your daily life or does it mostly focus on recruiting people for important roles at church? Are there creative ways to honor how people live their faith in their daily lives—when they are not at church?

3. The final portion of the liturgy is the Sending rite. Though it is the shortest of the four sections (Gathering, Word, Meal, Sending), it is no less important. Reflect on creative ways to emphasize the Sending in your community. Would this be the place for announcements or special ministry moments? How can the worshipping community embrace a mission spirituality of being sent?

10

Augmented Reality

Being There

I AM TRYING TO be less binary. We are conditioned to see everything as either this or that. Politics is more partisan than ever. We bifurcate spirituality from religion. The popular Myers-Briggs Type Indicator categorizes people as introverts or extroverts, thinkers or feelers. We delineate something as good or bad, helpful or harmful, worthy or irrelevant.

After reading this book thus far, you may sense I have a bias. Though the wonders of technology leave me awestruck, I have deep concerns that the growth of digitization means losing things essential to being human. Such a nuanced view leads me to recall the Lutheran principle of *simul justus et peccato*r. It means that—because of God's grace—we are simultaneously saint and sinner, justified and turned inward on the self. It is the *simul* that I want to focus on. Technology is morally neutral. Many things about our e-lives are exciting and yield previously unimagined possibilities for us. Simultaneously I believe there are new threats that undermine our ability to be attentive to the rich and wondrous experience of being human.

Though I owned my first computer a little over thirty years ago, it has only been ten years since the iPhone was introduced in 2007. By 2011 I was reading books that explored the downside to the ever-expanding digitization of daily life. For the next several years—as a part of my Doctor of Ministry studies—I read, reflected, and wrote on this topic from various liturgical, theological, technological, and social perspectives. Since then, articles and books on technology continue to proliferate, more of them with a psychological bent than a theological one. While writing this concluding chapter, three books came to my attention that illustrate the *simul* reality I named above.

The first book is a corrective to the pessimistic attitude some spiritual writers have toward technology. Theologian Deanna Thompson, a stage IV cancer survivor, was at first skeptical about many of the same things that concern me. Yet, in the midst of her illness Thompson received deep and authentic care and support through online relationships. Thompson argues that making a clear delineation between the "virtual world" and the "real world" is unhelpful. She believes that the virtual world *is* real and is bound up with what is essentially human, and thus a true extension of ourselves. Thompson writes that sometimes she was better able to express her vulnerability, fears, and tears digitally than in person. She makes the bold claim that the virtual body of Christ can assist us in attending to the suffering and pain that fills our lives, especially among the weakest members among us.[1]

A book by Adam Alter falls on the opposite side of the spectrum. Alter suggests that we are addicted to technology primarily not because we lack willpower; rather, creators of apps and programs have designed them to break down our self-regulation. The irresistible power that smartphones and computers have over us is more additive than anything in recent human history.[2] Ironically, we get so hooked that some people turn to apps like Moment to help monitor their screen time. For example, Alter predicted that he was using his phone about an hour a day and picking it up approximately forty times daily. In actuality the Moment app revealed that he averaged closer to three hours of phone use a day, handling the phone about a hundred times daily.[3] In addition, Alter reports that between 2000 and 2012 our average attention span has decreased from twelve seconds to eight seconds, while he playfully adds that the attention span of a goldfish is nine seconds.[4]

Finally, Israeli author Yuval Harari argues that people used to pray to the gods to spare them from war, poverty, and famine. Now we believe that science can solve any problem if we gain more knowledge or skill. Rather than valuing trust in a Messiah to save us, Harari argues that a geek in Silicon Valley could very well solve the problem of old age and death. He argues that for many people today, the old myths and the old gods are dead. The realm of technology is what is powerful. Once we turned to priests, rabbis, and shamans; now we turn to engineers. This new "techno-religion," as Harari names it, makes the kind of promises earlier associated with

1. Thompson, *Virtual Body of Christ*, 3–50.
2. Alter, *Irresistible*, 3–4.
3. Ibid., 14.
4. Ibid., 28.

religion. It offers happiness, justice, and immortality here on earth. Salvation comes through algorithms and genetic engineering. Harari foresees the day when a brain-computer interface will enable people to move from healing the sick to upgrading the bodies of the healthy. And since not everyone be able to afford these designer bodies, economic inequality will morph into biological inequality.[5]

In addition, many scientists say we have now entered a new geological epoch: the Anthropocene, the age of the human. Humanity is controlling nature. We use the earth's resources for our benefit without regard for other animals, plants, or ecosystems. We believe and act as if *we* are the center of everything.

In these three recent books, one author (Deanna Thompson) is advocating a more positive approach to the role of virtuality as a means of social networking, while the other two authors (Adam Alter and Yuval Harari) are expressing serious concerns about what human beings are losing through our evolving relationship with technology. These conflicting views illustrate the *simul* that I desire to hold in tension, yet it is my own reservations about what we are losing in the digital age that lead me to propose the role of worship as a moderating factor and as a spiritual practice.

Augmented Reality

The capabilities of the smartphone in my hand are simply dazzling. If one definition of a god is whom or what we turn to for guidance or in times of need, our phones have taken on godlike qualities. Returning to my nonbinary evaluation, this new world feels both awesome and terrifying to me. I believe the way we as a species maneuver through the moral, spiritual, and social implications of these technological advances will be integral to who we will become as human beings. As I hope has been clear throughout this book, I argue that religious and spiritual leaders have a crucial role in these conversations and deliberations. Despite the concerns that some people are raising about technology, we aren't going to go back to a previous time. Our perpetual connection to the Internet is the new normal. Insightful voices within a variety of disciplines are asking: What now? How shall we live? How do we incorporate the best of digitization while being cautious, seeking moderation when appropriate and balance when needed?

---

5. Harari, interview with author. See Harari, *Homo Deus*.

Augmented reality may be an appropriate way to describe our current relationship with the Internet. In the early years of the Internet, we had to go online to check our email or find something on the Web. Now most of us are nearly always connected. And it seems almost certain that the future will bring a constant tethering between human beings and the Internet. One website defines augmented reality (AR) as "an emerging technology that digitizes interaction with the physical world."[6] Wearable technology is the first sign of this new reality. Though I fear and resist a device that connects me to the Internet while being lodged in or on my body, I certainly marvel at what my smartphone does for me in a single day. A cadre of apps allows me to check email, obtain a weather forecast, get automated directions while driving, track my health and exercise, provide me with a timer and bells while meditating, stream an endless supply of music and movies, download documents I have created, take and edit photographs, adjust a thermostat remotely, serve as a scanning device, translate a phrase in a foreign language, post travel reports while halfway across the world, and FaceTime with loved ones hundreds or thousands of miles away. And this is only my short list. Though the quality of our daily lives is and will be further enhanced in many ways through such augmented reality, I have deep concerns about the implications for our spiritual ability to pay attention and live in the present moment. Thus, in these final reflections, I am going to employ the term *augmented reality* to suggest that an incarnational, sacramental spirituality arising from corporate worship also gives us a different lens for our lives. If by *augment* we mean to enlarge, increase, and expand, my use of *augmented reality* corresponds with what I have been advocating throughout this book: a spirituality that enhances our being in the present moment, being in our bodies, and being on the earth. My central thesis could be rephrased in this way: attending worship and participating in a faith community provide an augmented reality for our busy, distracted, and disjointed Internet-connected lives.

In Church

For my entire life I have consistently loved going to church. The meaning I derive from worship, however, has varied depending on my age and context. In all times and seasons, whether my theology was conservative or progressive, and whether my life circumstances were filled with struggle or

6. http://www.augmentedreality.org.

contentment, the rituals of the Christian faith have continued to nourish and sustain me for the journey of becoming the human person God calls me to be. I understand many of the reasons that people reject organized religion. I have heard these stories throughout my ministry, especially since I have been a pastor in communities where LGBTQ persons and others have felt hurt and excluded. I have also heard people tell me of sermons that they heard in previous churches that were judgmental, boring, or irrelevant. I am sad to hear these experiences. Yet in a fragmented, fearful, and anxious world, I still contend that—at its best—gathering together in community around rituals and practices opens our minds and hearts to a source of unimaginable beauty and grace. I long for a renewal of worship that unleashes the gospel in palpable ways.

It is not that we meet God solely in sacred places, but without intentional time away from our 24/7 reality of work and streaming data it is increasingly difficult for us to sense divine purpose and hope for our lives and for the world. It is true that in the past religion seemed too disconnected from everyday life and religious leaders talked too much about finding God solely in church. Now it seems that the pendulum has swung too far in the other direction: if God is found primarily in the ordinary, religion can seem archaic and irrelevant. Yet religious ritual retains a critical role in our lives. Ritual, however, forces us to stop in our tracks.[7] Holy places become a *focusing lens* for us, in which "one enters a marked-off space in which, at least in principle, nothing is accidental; everything, at least potentially, is of significance . . . The ordinary (which remains ordinary to the observer's eye, wholly ordinary) becomes significant, becomes sacred, simply by *being there*. It becomes sacred by having our attention directed to it in a special way."[8] With such a sacramental view of life, we choose not to distinguish between what is sacred and what is profane. We use earthly elements to communicate spiritual meaning. Thus, a place or thing takes on a holy purpose or meaning only when it is seen in relation to something else. For example, a bird makes its way into a church and sees what some call "holy water," yet to the bird this water is merely for its own drinking or bathing.[9] When Christians use water, bread, wine, and oil, these ordinary things take on spiritual and extraordinary significance. It is not simply water in the font that is holy, but the focusing lens of ritual helps us to look on all lakes,

7. Driver, *Magic of Ritual*, 48.

8. Smith, *Imagining Religion*, 54–55.

9. Ibid., 55.

rivers, streams, and oceans as holy. Sharing the bread and wine of the Eucharist makes sacred all our gatherings around tables.

We need the focusing lens of worship to provide an augmented sense of reality in contrast to the narratives of advertising, politics, and the media that shape most of our lives. Amid the individualism so prevalent in our culture, we are brought back to community and reminded of our baptismal call to serve in the world. When abundant screen time distracts us from interacting with people in real time, in worship we are brought back to embodiment and the gifts and challenges of human mortality and finitude. Celebrating the Eucharist each week forms us in the paschal mystery and reminds us of our participation in the ongoing project of death and resurrection. I can think of few other human endeavors that continue to beckon us to embrace the full spectrum of what it means to be human. While the word *irresistible* is being used to describe our relationship to technology, I deeply long for worship to hook people with a gospel that offers wholeness, meaning, purpose, and hope. My life's work has been devoted to the renewal of liturgy—not for its own sake, but because I believe the augmented reality of irresistible grace and healing we celebrate in church is a source of transformation not only for individuals, but for the world.

In the Moment

Most of us take photographs to capture human moments so that we can remember them—and possibly relive them—years into the future. We have all noticed vacationers snapping endless photographs. Before selfies we could never be *in* the pictures we took. Yet when we pay more attention to the taking of pictures than the cool experience we are supposedly having, we are never *in* the present moment either. You've probably heard that the best camera these days is the one we have on our smartphone. Now that we can take countless pictures—and even include ourselves in selfies—some are wondering whether we are taking so many pictures that most of them will never even be looked at. Add the plethora of photographs to the abundance of books, movies, television shows, songs, and other media that can be downloaded instantly, and it becomes increasingly difficult to choose something to watch, read, or listen to, and then actually give our full attention to it. Who knows? Another click may bring something better.

No wonder people are turning to meditation and mindfulness to help them live more fully in the present moment. I have practiced meditation for thirty years, though with varying degrees of regularity. When my spiritual director encouraged me to try this unfamiliar practice, she suggested that merely showing up brought its own benefits. Even when my mind wanders or I wonder what I am getting out of it, I trust that the practice of meditation is having effects on me that I do not see. My spiritual director's hope that I simply show up for meditation isn't that different from the desire I have that people would simply show up for worship. Both are spiritual *disciplines*, after all.

I now know that, due to the brain's neuroplasticity, meditation can bring about positive consequences on both body and mind. I find myself turning to my breath in times of stress or worry. The first mantra that the same spiritual director taught me often returns to me as well: "May I be filled with your loving-kindness. May I be filled with your peace." As much as I believe meditation—and similar practices like yoga—can affect my physical and emotional health, there is another benefit. Like religious ritual, meditation is another *focusing lens*. By focusing on the breath, and simply noticing thoughts and other distractions, I am learning to be more fully alive, practicing letting go (of thoughts and attachments), and seeking to be more attentive to the present moment and more open to the gift of life itself. For me that means trying to slow down even though my brain is always on the move. Mindfulness reminds me of the gift of doing one thing at a time—whether cooking, eating, washing dishes, or folding clothes. Though it seems more efficient to listen to a podcast while I go running—and I sometimes do—I also know that my best and most creative thinking happens when my body is moving and I am free to simply be in the moment.

Though this book is focused mostly on corporate worship, it is imperative that I name the importance of individual spiritual practices as well. As you can tell, I am optimistic that participating in the liturgy offers us an augmented reality that can provide meaning and purpose for our everyday lives. But I must also admit that one hour a week of worship—or even less than that for many people today—is likely not enough to counter how we are formed through constant connection to the Internet. Therefore, I would advocate for a combination of corporate worship and individual spiritual practices of choice. As the ancients teach us, the ultimate goal is openness to the present moment.

"Where shall I look for Enlightenment?" the disciple asked.

"Here," the elder said.

"When will it happen?" the disciple wanted to know.

"It is happening right now," the elder said.

"Then why don't I experience it?" the disciple asked.

And the elder answered, "Because you do not look."

"But what should I look for?" the disciple wanted to know.

And the elder smiled and answered, "Nothing. Just look."

"But at what?" the disciple insisted.

"Anything your eyes alight upon," the elder continued.

"Well, then, must I look in a special kind of way?" the disciple asked.

"No," the elder said.

"Why ever not?" the disciple persisted.

And the elder said quietly, "Because to look you must be here. The problem is that you are mostly somewhere else."[10]

In Everything

Benedictine spirituality—like much of recent spiritual writing—invites us to see God in all things. Many authors observe that we are living in a unique and rich time of spiritual renewal and transformation. A thread that I see in much reflection today is this: everything belongs and everything is connected. Globalism—coupled with the ability to be connected virtually via the Internet to someone across the ocean—opens vistas previously unimagined. The spiritual task today is to see the divine in everything. We have heard that human bodies are made of the same substance as the stars. That means our human-made computers and cell phones also share the same atomic makeup as the earth, and thus our bodies. When I talk about being more connected to the earth, I must grapple with the fact that our devices are made up of the earth as well.

My primary concern, though, is not the fact of our connection to technological devices, but the reality that the magnitude of this connection often inhibits our ability to be attentive to all that it means to be human—especially the challenging emotions of loneliness, emptiness, loss, and grief. If personal transformation comes from our encounter with the struggles of life, we need time and space to be with all that is, including the most difficult aspects of being human. Poet David Whyte wisely states that we have difficulty putting down our gadgets or turning off the television because it seems as if the awareness of mortality is undermining us and is leading to

10. Chittister, *Wisdom Distilled from the Daily*, 201–2.

our demise. Yet he adds that this is precisely the truth of human existence that steers us "towards this richer, deeper place that doesn't get corroborated very much in our everyday outer world."[11] We all struggle to be here, to be with all that is. Incarnation ultimately means to be present here and now—to be present in our human bodies. When we accept this invitation, we more clearly realize that we are simultaneously a mortal human being and fully alive. Whyte asks: Will you show up to live as "the full citizen of vulnerability, loss, and disappearance, which you have no choice about?"[12] Whether celebrating the Eucharist, the liturgy of Ash Wednesday, or a funeral, the mystery of faith is connected to the mystery of being human.

At their best, religious rituals and spiritual practices provide the lens of an augmented reality, revealing what it means to be human—which is all too easy to miss amid the pace and patterns of our digital lives. If the holy is revealed in sacred space and time, and in our bodily experience of each day, then we have much to learn from the cycle of life with all its twists and turns: from birth and death, work and sleep, sexuality and illness; from the complexity of human emotion, whether joy, curiosity, sadness, or depression. When technology augments our bodily experience of being human with its many shades and contours, there is reason to be grateful. When technology inhibits or distracts us from paying attention to nature, to other people, or to the deep longings in our hearts, it is time to step back and assess what modifications are needed in our lifestyles and routines. We hold the *simul* in tension: acknowledging the gifts that technological advances bring to our lives while confronting the dangers and excesses as well.

In and for the World

Any body there? I asked at the outset. Bodies matter. The earth matters. The common good matters. Participating in the liturgy is a curriculum that teaches the purposes of God, the goodness of life, and a pattern for our own life and death. But there is more. Worship is transformational because it leads us to embody the mission of God in and for the world. True service will demand human bodies that recognize the suffering and pain of other human bodies. If liturgy forms us to appreciate the wonder and vulnerability of our own bodies, it sends us to tend to both the physical and spiritual needs of our neighbors. Posting a message of condolence online is not the

11. Whyte, "Conversational Nature of Reality."

12. Ibid.

same as embracing someone in grief or showing up at someone's door with food or flowers. Signing an online petition is not the same as personal encounters with fellow human beings in need, as important as the former may be.

Christian practice is centered in an incarnate God who shares fully all that it means to be human—taking on a body and responding to the bodily needs of others. It is easy to miss this augmented reality due to the distractions of our digital lives. The two great commandments—love of God and neighbor—take us out of our selfie preoccupation and remind us that our GPS dot does not signify that we are the center of the world, but that we are called to serve wherever we are. As human beings continue to merge with machines, many wonder whether their lives make any difference in the grand scheme of things. The baptismal life—a holy vocation in which the common good is served through our various roles as parents, spouses, friends, students, neighbors, workers, volunteers, and community members—shows that we do make a difference. The various gifts and passions of the community are joined to God's desire for shalom in and for the world.

If paying attention is the spiritual task of our time, we need reminders of what truly matters and what holds meaning amid all the clamors that mark our 24/7 digital age. When we find the draw of screen time irresistible, consider how our bodies and souls long for unplugged times of spiritual refreshment and beauty through worship, encounters in nature, and bodily recreation. There is no question that I believe in the many benefits of going to church. *Anybody there?* My prayer is that as embodied human beings we will be fully present at church, in the moment, and in all that is. We will need preachers and teachers that make the connections between worship and daily life. With a sense of augmented reality, we have a new lens for life: seeing everything and everyone as an icon of the divine. Going to church leads to *being* the church in the world. Fully present to the joys and sorrows of life, we are *there*, even as we journey into an unknown future.

Bibliography

Aboujaoude, Elias. *Virtually You: The Dangerous Powers of the E-Personality.* New York: Norton, 2012.

Agger, Ben. "iTime: Labor and Life in a Smartphone Era." *Time and Society* 20 (2011) 119–36.

Alder, Adam. *Irresistible: The Rise of Addictive Technology and the Business of Keeping Us Hooked.* New York: Penguin, 2017.

Anderson, E. Byron. "A Body for the Spirit in the World: Eucharist, Epiclesis, and Ethics." *Worship* 85 (March 2011) 98–116.

————. "Liturgy: Writing Faith in the Body." *Liturgical Ministry* 20 (Fall 2011) 172–77.

Arikha, Noga. "The Internet and the Loss of Tranquility." In *Is the Internet Changing the Way You Think?: The Net's Impact on Our Minds and Future,* 41–43. New York: Harper Perennial, 2011.

Bass, Diana Butler. *Christianity After Religion: The End of Church and the Birth of a New Spiritual Awakening.* New York: HarperOne, 2012.

————. *Grounded: Finding God in the World—a Spiritual Revolution.* New York: HarperCollins, 2015.

Bass, Dorothy. *Receiving the Day: Christian Practices for Opening the Gift of Time.* San Francisco: Jossey-Bass, 2000.

Beaudoin, Tom. *Virtual Faith: The Irreverent Spiritual Quest of Generation X.* San Francisco: Jossey-Bass, 2000.

Berry, Wendell. "Whatever Is Foreseen in Joy." In *This Day: Collected and New Sabbath Poems,* 20. Berkeley, CA: Counterpoint, 2013.

Bieler, Andrea, and Luise Schottroff. *The Eucharist: Bodies, Bread, and Resurrection.* Minneapolis: Fortress, 2007.

Bliese, Richard H., and Craig Van Gelder. *The Evangelizing Church: A Lutheran Contribution.* Minneapolis: Augsburg Fortress, 2005.

Borgmann, Albert. *Technology and the Character of Contemporary Life: A Philosophical Inquiry.* Chicago: University of Chicago Press, 1987.

Bria, Ion. *The Liturgy After the Liturgy: Mission and Witness from an Orthodox Perspective.* Geneva: World Council of Churches, 1996.

Briggs, Sheila. "Digital Bodies and the Transformation of the Flesh." In *Toward a Theology of Eros: Transfiguring Passion at the Limits of Discipline*, edited by Virginia Burrus and Catherine Keller, 153–68. New York: Fordham University Press, 2006.

Brooks, David. "How to Fix Politics." *New York Times*, April 12, 2016.

Brown, Frank Burch. "Aesthetics: An Essay on Aesthetics and the Theologian." ARTS 3 (Fall 1990) 11–14

Brubaker, Leslie. *Vision and Meaning in Ninth-Century Byzantium: Images as Exegesis in the Homilies of Gregory of Nazianzus*. Cambridge, UK: Cambridge University Press, 1999.

Brueggemann, Walter. *Sabbath as Resistance: Saying No to the Culture of Now*. Louisville: Westminster John Knox, 2014.

Brugh, Lorraine, and Gordon Lathrop. *The Sunday Assembly: Using Evangelical Lutheran Worship*. Minneapolis: Augsburg Fortress, 2008.

Brunk, Timothy. "Consumer Culture and the Body: Chauvet's Perspective." *Worship* 82 (2008) 290–310.

Burns, Stephen. "Yearning without Saying a Word: Unembarrassed Presiding in Liturgy." *Worship* 85 (2011) 2–16.

Bushkovsky, Dennis, et al, eds. *Go Make Disciples: An Invitation to Baptismal Living*. Minneapolis: Augsburg Fortress, 2012.

Capon, Robert Farrar. *The Supper of the Lamb: A Culinary Reflection*. Garden City, NY: Doubleday, 1969.

Carr, Nicholas. *The Shallows: What the Internet Is Doing to Our Brains*. New York: Norton, 2010.

Chauvet, Louise-Marie, and Francois Kabasele Lumbala, eds. *Liturgy and the Body*. Concilium 1995/3. London: SCM, 1995.

Chittister, Joan. *Wisdom Distilled from the Daily: Living the Rule of St. Benedict Today*. New York: HarperCollins, 1990.

Christian Worship: Unity in Cultural Diversity. LWF Studies. Geneva: Department for Theology and Studies, Lutheran World Federation, 1996.

Ckuj, Simon. "Praying with Icons." http://bne.catholic.net.au/data/portal/00005057/0000/005/283/content/01874001336103212646.pdf.

Claxton, Guy. "Corporal Thinking." *Chronicle of Higher Education* 62 (2015) 19.

Cope, Stephen. *The Great Work of Your Life: A Guide for the Journey to Your True Calling*. New York: Bantam, 2012.

Dawn, Marva. *A Royal Waste of Time: The Splendor of Worshiping God and Being Church for the World*. Grand Rapids: Eerdmans, 1999.

Detweiler, Craig. *iGods: How Technology Shapes Our Spiritual and Social Lives*. Grand Rapids: Brazos, 2013.

Doestoevsky, Fyodor. *The Idiot*. Translated by Thomas Epstein. Russian Academy Edition. Leningrad, 1972.

Drescher, Elizabeth. *Tweet If You ♥ Jesus: Practicing Church in the Digital Reformation*. Kindle ed. New York: Morehouse, 2011.

Driver, Tom. *The Magic of Ritual: Our Need for Liberating Rites that Transform Our Lives and Our Communities*. San Francisco: Harper, 1991.

Duckworth, Jessicah Krey. *Wide Welcome: How the Unsettling Presence of Newcomers Can Save the Church*. Minneapolis: Fortress, 2013.

Duffy, Stephen J. *The Dynamics of Grace: Perspectives in Theological Anthropology*. New Theology Series 3. Collegeville, MN: Liturgical, 1993.

Eiesland, Nancy. *The Disabled God: Toward a Liberatory Theology of Disability.* Nashville: Abingdon, 1994.

Empereur, James L. "Is Liturgy an Art Form?" *Liturgical Ministry* 5 (1996) 97–107.

Evangelical Lutheran Worship. Minneapolis: Augsburg Fortress, 2006.

Farwell, James. *This Is the Night: Suffering, Salvation, and the Liturgies of Holy Week.* New York: T. & T. Clark, 2005.

Gaillardetz, Richard. *Transforming Our Days: Spirituality, Community, and Liturgy in a Technological Culture.* New York: Crossroad, 2000.

Garcia-Rivera, Alejandro. *The Community of the Beautiful.* Collegeville, MN: Liturgical, 1999.

Garfield, Simon. "Mapping a History of the World, and Our Place In It." Interview on *All Things Considered,* NPR, January 7, 2013. http://www.npr.org/2013/01/07/168090325/mapping-a-history-of-the-world-and-our-place-in-it.

Gregarsen, Hans Henrik, ed. *Incarnation: On the Scope and Depth of Christology.* Minneapolis: Fortress, 2015.

Griffith, Colleen M. "Spirituality and the Body." In *Bodies of Worship: Explorations in Theory and Practice,* edited by Bruce Morrill, 67–84. Collegeville, MN: Liturgical, 1999.

Harari, Yuval Noah. *Homo Deus: A Brief History of Tomorrow.* San Francisco: Harper, 2017.

———. Interview by Azeem Azhar. *Exponential View* (podcast), March 2, 2017. https://soundcloud.com/exponentialview/homo-deus-a-conversation-between-yuval-harari-and-azeem-azhar.

Harris, Michael. *The End of Absence: Reclaiming What We've Lost in a World of Constant Connection.* New York: Current, 2014.

Hayles, N. Katherine. *How We Became Posthuman: Virtual Bodies in Cybernetics, Literature, and Informatics.* Chicago: University of Chicago Press, 1999.

Hays, Ed. *Pray All Ways: A Book for Daily Worship Using All Your Senses.* Notre Dame, IN: Ave Maria, 2007.

Hefner, Philip. Interview with Susan Barreto. Part 1 of 2. Lutheran Alliance for Faith, Science and Technology, July 2011. http://luthscitech.org/phil-hefner-part-one-evangelical-lutheran-church-in-america/.

Hefner, Philip, Susan Baretto, and Ann Milliken Pedersen. *Our Bodies Are Selves.* Kindle ed. Eugene, OR: Cascade, 2015.

Heschel, Abraham. *The Sabbath: Its Meaning for the Modern Man.* New York: Farrar, Straus and Girouz, 1979.

"Holy Trinity, Chicago, Illinois, USA." *Mystery Worshipper* (blog), 2969, Ship of Fools, January 10, 2016. http://www.shipoffools.com/mystery/2016/2969.html.

Hopkins, Gerard Manley. "Spring and Fall." In *Poems and Prose of Gerard Manley Hopkins,* 50. New York: Penguin Classics, 1985.

Hovda, Robert. *The Amen Corner.* Collegeville, MN: Liturgical, 1994.

———. *Strong, Loving, and Wise: Presiding in Liturgy.* Collegeville, MN: Liturgical, 1980.

Huck, Gabe, ed. *Toward Ritual Transformation: Remembering Robert W. Hovda.* Collegeville, MN: Liturgical, 2003.

Kearney, Richard. "Losing Our Touch." *New York Times,* August 31, 2014.

Kemp, Martin. *From Christ to Coke: How Image Becomes Icon.* Oxford: Oxford University Press, 2011.

Kreider, Alan, and Eleanor Kreider. *Worship and Mission After Christendom*. Scottdale, PA: Herald, 2011.

Kreider, Tim. "You Are Going to Die." *New York Times*, January 20, 2013.

Lathrop, Gordon W. *Holy People: A Liturgical Ecclesiology*. Minneapolis: Fortress, 1999.

Long, Kimberly Bracken. *The Worshiping Body: The Art of Leading Worship*. Louisville, KY: Westminster John Knox, 2009.

Long, Thomas G. *Accompany Them with Singing: The Christian Funeral*. Louisville: Westminster John Knox, 2009.

Lose, David J. "An Emboldening Thought." . . . *In the Meantime* (blog), October 16, 2014. http://www.davidlose.net/2014/10/an-emboldening-thought/.

————. *Preaching at the Crossroads: Now the World—and Our Preaching—Is Changing*. Minneapolis: Fortress, 2013.

————. "10 Things the Church Can Learn from the Apple Store." Blog. May 18, 2012.

Lovas, András. "Mission-Shaped Liturgy." *International Review of Mission* 95 (2006) 352–58.

Luther, Martin. "Against the Heavenly Prophets in Manners of Images and Sacraments." In *Luther's Works*, vol. 40, edited by Jaroslav Pelikan and Helmut Lehmann. Philadelphia and St. Louis: Fortress and Concordia, 1955–85.

Lutheran Alliance for Science and Technology. http://luthscitech.org.

Lutheran Book of Worship. Minneapolis: Augsburg, 1978.

Lyon, David. *Jesus in Disneyland: Religion in Postmodern Times*. Malden, MA: Polity, 2000.

Martin, Linette. *Sacred Doorways: A Beginner's Guide to Icons*. Brewster, MA: Paraclete, 2002.

McCurley, Foster. *Go in Peace, Serve the Lord: The Social Ministry of the Church*. Minneapolis, Augsburg Fortress, 2000.

Mercadante, Linda A. *Beliefs without Borders: Inside the Minds of the Spiritual but Not Religious*. New York: Oxford University Press, 2014.

Merton, Thomas. *No Man Is an Island*. New York: Harcourt Brace Jovanovich, 1955.

Miller, Vincent. "Taking Consumer Culture Seriously." *Horizons* 27 (2000) 276–95.

————. "The Liturgy and Popular Culture." *Liturgical Ministry* 15 (2006) 161–70.

Mitchell, Nathan. "A Trinity of Themes." *Worship* 86 (2012) 71–84.

————. "Being Good and Being Beautiful." *Worship* 74 (2000) 550–58.

Moe-Lobeda, Cynthia. *Public Church: For the Life of the World*. Minneapolis: Augsburg Fortress, 2004.

Murphy, Nancey. "Human Nature: Historical, Scientific, and Religious Issues." In *What Ever Happened to the Soul?: Scientific and Theological Portraits of Human Nature*, edited by Warren S. Brown, Nancey Murphy, and H. Newton Malony, 1–21. Minneapolis: Fortress, 1998.

Pew Forum on Religion & Public Life. *"Nones" on the Rise: One-in-Five Adults Have No Religious Affiliation*. October 2012. http://www.pewforum.org/2012/10/09/nones-on-the-rise/.

O'Donahue, John. *Beauty: The Invisible Embrace*. New York: HarperCollins, 2004.

Peterson, Eugene. *Leap Over a Wall: Earthy Spirituality for Everyday Christians*. San Francisco: HarperSanFrancisco, 1997.

Pieper, Joseph. *Leisure: The Basis of Culture*. Translated by Alexander Dru. San Francisco: Ignatius, 2009.

Principles for Worship. Renewing Worship 2. Minneapolis: Augsburg Fortress, 2002. Available online at http://download.elca.org/ELCA%20Resource%20Repository/Principles_for_Worship.pdf.

Putnam, Robert. *Bowling Alone: The Collapse and Revival of American Community.* New York: Simon and Schuster, 2000.

Putnam, Robert, and David Campbell. *American Grace: How Religion Divides and Unites Us.* New York: Simon and Schuster, 2010.

Rabi'a. "O My Lord, If I Worship You." In *Women in Praise of the Sacred: 43 Centuries of Spiritual Poetry by Women,* translated by Jane Hirshfield, 44. New York: Harper Collins, 1974.

Rahner, Karl. *Foundations of Christian Faith.* Translated by William V. Dych. New York: Seabury, 1978.

Rappaport, Roy A. *Ritual and Religion in the Making of Humanity.* Cambridge: Cambridge University Press, 1999.

Rendle, Gil. *Doing the Math of Mission: Fruit, Faithfulness, and Metrics.* Lanham, MD: Rowman and Littlefield, 2014.

Rice, Charles. *The Embodied Word: Preaching as Art and Liturgy.* Minneapolis: Fortress, 1991.

Rilke, Rainer Maria. *Letters to a Young Poet.* Translated by Stephen Mitchell. New York: Modern Library, 2001.

Robinson, Ken. "Do Schools Kill Creativity?" TED Talk, February 2006.

Rohr, Richard. "Utterly Humbled by Mystery." *This I Believe*, Morning Edition, NPR, December 18, 2006. http://www.npr.org/templates/story/story.php?storyId=6631954.

Rosen, Larry D. *iDisorder: Understanding Our Obsession with Technology and Overcoming Its Hold on Us.* New York: Palgrave Macmillan, 2012.

Rushkoff, Douglas. *Present Shock: When Everything Happens Now.* New York: Current, 2013.

Saliers, Don E. "Beauty and Terror." In *Minding the Spirit: The Study of Christian Spirituality*, edited by Elizabeth A. Dreyer and Mark S. Burrows, 303–13. Baltimore: Johns Hopkins University Press, 2005.

———. *Worship as Theology: Foretaste of Glory Divine.* Nashville: Abingdon, 1994.

Schmemann, Alexander. *For the Life of the World.* Crestwood, NY: St. Vladimir's Seminary Press, 2000.

Shlain, Leonard. *The Alphabet Versus the Goddess: The Conflict between Word and Image.* New York: Viking, 1998.

Senn, Frank. *Embodied Liturgy: Lessons in Christian Ritual.* Minneapolis: Fortress, 2016.

Small, Gary, and Gigi Vorgan. *iBrain: Surviving the Technological Alteration of the Modern Mind.* New York: HarperCollins, 2009.

Smith, Jonathan. *Imagining Religion: From Babylon to Jonestown.* Chicago: University of Chicago Press, 1982.

Spinks, Bryan D. *The Worship Mall: Contemporary Responses to Contemporary Culture.* New York: Church, 2011.

Stephens, Mitchell. *The Rise of the Image, and the Fall of the Word.* New York: Oxford University Press, 1998.

Stewart, Benjamin. "Ash Wednesday: Understanding the Day." In *Worship Guidebook for Lent and the Three Days*, edited by Robert Buckley Farlee and Scott Weidler, 18–23. Minneapolis: Augsburg Fortress, 2009.

Stuempfle, Herman. *Preaching Law and Gospel.* Philadelphia: Fortress, 1978

Swanson, Mark. "New Realities, New Thinking since 1990." In *Engaging Others, Knowing Ourselves: A Lutheran Calling in a Multi-Religious World*, edited by Carol Schersten LaHurd et al., 25–44. Minneapolis: Lutheran University Press, 2016.

Thompson, Deanna. *The Virtual Body of Christ in a Suffering World*. Memphis: Abingdon, 2016.

Thoreau, Henry David. *Walden*. Boston: Beacon, 2004.

Torvend, Samuel. *Luther and the Hungry Poor: Gathered Fragments*. Minneapolis: Fortress, 2008.

———. "Touch Me and See: A Resurrection of the Body in Church?" *CrossAccent: Journal of the Association of Lutheran Church Musicians* 21 (2013) 18–25.

Turkle, Sherry. *Reclaiming Conversation: The Power of Talk in a Digital Age*. New York: Penguin, 2015.

Turner, Victor Witter. *The Ritual Process: Structure and Anti-Structure*. Chicago: Aldine, 1969.

Viladesau, Richard. *Theology and the Arts: Encountering God through Music, Art, and Rhetoric*. New York: Paulist, 2000.

Vryhof, David. *Living Intentionally: Creating a Personal Rule of Life. Monastic Wisdom for Everyday Living*. Cambridge, MA: Society of Saint John the Evangelist, 2011. http://ssje.org/5.pdf/cowleypdf/2011%20Summer%20Insert.pdf.

Wagner, Rachel. *Godwired: Religion, Ritual, and Virtual Reality*. New York: Routledge, 2011.

Wajcman, Judy. *Pressed for Time: The Acceleration of Life in Digital Capitalism*. Chicago: University of Chicago Press, 2015.

Weil, Simone. *The Simone Weil Reader*. Edited by George A. Panichas. New York: David McKay Co., 1977.

Whyte, David. "The Conversational Nature of Reality." Interview with Krista Tippett. *On Being*, April 7, 2016. Transcript. https://onbeing.org/programs/david-whyte-the-conversational-nature-of-reality/.

Wuthnow, Robert. *After the Baby Boomers: How Twenty- and Thirty-Somethings Are Shaping the Future of American Religion*. Princeton, NJ: Princeton University Press, 2010.

Zimmerman, Joyce. "Beauty and the Beast: Criteria for Artful Liturgy." In *Postmodern Worship and the Arts*, edited by Doug Adams and Michael E. Moynahan, 21–32. San Jose, CA: Resource, 2002.

Zsupan-Jerome, Daniella. "Virtual Presence as Real Presence?: Sacramental Theology and Digital Culture in Dialogue." *Worship* 89 (November 2015) 526–42.

66899770R00081

Made in the USA
Lexington, KY
28 August 2017